A   WHOLE   NEW   WORLD:

LIFE   AFTER   BETHANY

Smyth & Helwys Publishing, Inc.
6316 Peake Road
Macon, Georgia 31210-3960
1-800-747-3016
©2005 by Smyth & Helwys Publishing
All rights reserved.
Printed in the United States of America.

The paper used in this publication meets the minimum requirements of
American National Standard for Information Sciences—
Permanence of Paper for Printed Library Materials.
ANSI Z39.48–1984. (alk. paper)

Library of Congress Cataloging-in-Publication Data

Cartledge, Tony W.
A whole new world / by Tony and Jan Cartledge.
p. cm.
Includes bibliographical references.
ISBN 978-1-57312-448-5 (pbk. : alk. paper)
1. Children—Death—Religious aspects—Christianity.
2. Consolation.
3. Death—Religious aspects—Christianity.
4. Bereavement—Religious aspects—Christianity.
I. Cartledge, Jan.
II. Title.
BV4907.C37 2005
248.8'66'0922--dc22

2005006547

A   WHOLE   NEW   WORLD:

LIFE   AFTER   BETHANY

JAN   AND   TONY   CARTLEDGE

d e d i c a t i o n

All the words in this book, even multiplied ten thousand times, cannot express the depth of our love for Bethany or the place she has in our hearts. It is to her, of course, that we dedicate this book.

contents

preface

This is a book about loss and about life, about despair and hope, about darkness and dawn. It begins with a personal accounting of a parent's worst highway nightmare and ends along a winding road where happier dreams may still be found.

The central character in this story is Bethany Rush Cartledge, a sunny seven-year-old girl who dies in the first chapter but lives on every page.

Bethany was a charmer. With her short blond hair and snaggle-toothed grin, Bethany warmed the hearts of almost everyone she met. She was darling in a dress but most at home in a sweatshirt and jeans. She loved T-ball and bike riding, teddy bears and art projects, fish sticks and French fries. She could be a snuggle-bunny wanting to be held close, and a brave kindergartener climbing onto the school bus for the first time.

Bethany was big-hearted. She loved her mommy and daddy and her big brother Russ; she loved her grandparents and enjoyed spending time with them; she loved her church friends, her school friends, and her neighborhood friends. She loved her cats and cried when they died. When Duke, her grey tomcat, managed to get himself run over, Bethany curled him carefully in a big shoe box, buried him by the chimney, marked the spot with a cross, and planted a maple tree to remember him by.

Bethany was a child of faith. She looked forward to church time, learned eagerly from her teachers, sang joyfully in the children's choir, and proudly rang a little bell in the children's hand bell choir. At the conclusion of worship, when her pastor-father stepped from the pulpit to walk up the aisle during the benediction, Bethany would often slip out, wrap her arms around one leg, and walk with him into the vestibule. She asked good questions and believed in the goodness of God and the love of Jesus as only a child can.

A story from Bethany's short pilgrimage of faith provides an apt metaphor for what we have felt for these past eleven years, and for what we continued to feel as we wrote this book. One evening, as we sat around the dinner table when she was just two or three years old, Bethany wanted to say the blessing. She prayed, "Thank you, God, for living in my heart." Then, with a soft giggle, she added "Back and forth, back and forth, back and forth . . . ." We couldn't help but peek, and saw Bethany rocking back and forth in her chair, playing a game with God to see if He could keep up and stay in her heart as she moved about.

Now Bethany has moved into another world, a whole new world where her faith journey is complete, even as ours continues. Bethany's sweet smile and warm body are no longer with us. We confidently believe that her spirit rests with God, while we have been shaken and moved about in ways we never imagined. Yet, there has never been a moment in which we did not feel her presence in some way, firmly woven into the fiber of our own being through the warp and woof of memory and hope.

It is our prayer that the words yet to come in this book will offer encouragement and hope to others who know what it is to experience loss and stand at the threshold of a whole new world, wondering what comes next.

Jan and Tony Cartledge

acknowledgments

We teach our children to say "please" and "thank you," and we could not publish this book without expressing our thanks to so many people who have been instrumental in bringing it about.

Our son Samuel, for instance. He has been patient with his parents when one or the other would slip away to spend time in writing and remembering, giving attention to his sister's memory instead of his presence. He is a daily blessing to us and a constant reminder of God's goodness. Other family members were a mainstay to us, especially in the early days, and we remain grateful for their care.

We were exceedingly fortunate to have a loving family of faith who cared for us with compassion, maturity, and selflessness in the days following Bethany's death. Though we were two of the three "official" ministers at Woodhaven Baptist Church, our faith family literally lived out the church mantra of every member being a minister. They cooked for us, cleaned for us, and cried for us. They held our hands and blessed our hearts in countless ways.

Several close friends went above and beyond the call of duty in supporting us, not only in the immediate aftermath of Bethany's death, but in the months and years to follow. Janice Haywood, for example, has become more like a family member than a friend—so much so that we named our son Samuel Haywood Cartledge and asked Janice to be his godmother.

Sue Colenda and Robin Vines (now Penninger) both came with suitcases in hand and a willingness to stay as long as we needed them. Jill Keel was a frequent companion and an amazing listener who shared herself and her children with us. Norma Evans coordinated a bevy of church friends too numerous to name and ran a virtual restaurant from our kitchen for nearly a week. Months later, Phyllis Yelvington and some of her quilting friends turned several of Bethany's dresses into marvelous memory quilts.

Hal Melton kept the youth program going, Debbie Huskey was both secretary and friend, and Gene Moore stepped up to take on a far greater leadership role than he had planned on as part-time minister of music. Many other church members proved their mettle in providing a variety of ministries both in the church and in our home.

Minister friends were also a comfort. Jack Glasgow, pastor of Zebulon Baptist Church, assisted with the funeral and became our virtual pastor for a while. Friends from Tony's minister support group and colleagues from Jan's circle of youth minister friends were (and are) an encouragement. Sometimes ministry came from unexpected directions, such as the kindness we experienced from Fred Rogers and the friendship that developed.

Several friends and family members helped us clarify fuzzy memories by reading drafts of this book and commenting honestly. Steve Sumerel agreed to write a helpful and creative study guide for adults, while Janice Haywood and Hal Melton provided additional resources for helping children and youth deal with the reality of death. Their contributions make the book both better and more useful, and we are grateful for their efforts.

Likewise, we appreciate our friends and the editors at Smyth & Helwys Publishing who were willing to take on this project and to help us see it through.

This book begins with loss, but it is really about hope and faith that comes from a God who is bigger than death and all about life. For the life and hope we have in Him, we offer our most profound thanks.

One Morning in Time

Tony

On the day our daughter died, the world woke up and went about its business. That night, it went to sleep. But in the course of the morning, one thread in one small corner of the living world's fabric snapped. Our little Bethany encountered eternity, and we found ourselves in a whole new world.

January 18, 1994, dawned crisp and clear outside of Lincolnton, Georgia, a small town near the South Carolina line, some forty miles northwest of Augusta. Seven-year-old Bethany crawled out of the single bed in a room that once was mine, pushed the short, blond hair away from her face, and sat down for a breakfast of pancakes and bacon with "Mama Hollie" and "Daddy Bill." A rambunctious week with her Georgia grandparents, an extra benefit of her year-round school schedule, was coming to an end.

I had arrived the night before. My job was to bring Bethany back to our home near Raleigh, North Carolina, and she was ready to come home. With no prompting, Bethany traded her nightshirt for a white turtleneck and the purple windsuit she had gotten for Christmas, then brushed her snaggled teeth. While I loaded suitcases and toys into the trunk of our aging 1986 Oldsmobile Cutlass, Bethany was on the phone with Jan, letting her mommy know what time we were leaving and when to expect us home.

There is no straight road from Lincolnton to Raleigh, but the most direct route starts on Highway 378, cutting across South Carolina through McCormick, Saluda, and Lexington, turning east onto I-20 near Columbia. That was the road we traveled as Bethany waved good-bye to Mama Hollie and Daddy Bill, then launched into a bubbly description of her visit. I was most surprised to hear that our little tomboy had enjoyed playing dress-up one night, complete with makeup and jewelry.

We made a short stop at a bank in Lexington before taking I-20 through Columbia to Camden. There we cut across to Highway 1, a relatively straight two-lane road through the peach orchards and pine forests of upstate South Carolina. From there it winds through the Sandhills and into the Piedmont region of North Carolina, passing within four miles of our home.

The journey was nearly three hours old by the time we reached Highway 1, and it had begun to wear on us. We had run out of news from the week apart and exhausted our repertoire of travel games and knock-knock jokes. Bethany, sitting beside me in the front passenger seat, took off her sneakers and asked me to play a cassette tape of original music that Jan had recorded a couple of years earlier. My daughter and I shared a mutual love for her mother's clear and gentle singing voice, and we talked little as the tape ran its comforting course.

Jan's album came to an end as the road entered a large forest preserve of longleaf pines between the tiny crossroads towns of McBee and Patrick. We were both ready for a break from the road. Bethany had wanted to stop for lunch when we passed through Camden, but it was barely 11:00 AM at the time, and I had pressed on. I promised to stop at one of the fast food restaurants in Cheraw, less than an hour away.

A bit more than half of that hour had passed as we approached Middendorf, a loose collection of mostly mobile homes and a small gravestone company tucked between the highway and the pinewoods. The road was open and lightly traveled enough to allow the use of cruise control. I remember easing around a slower-moving dump truck near the bottom of a long incline. As we motored up the next hill and toward the hidden curve beyond it, Bethany announced that she wanted to stop at Hardee's for a lunch of fried chicken, and I told her that sounded like a fine plan.

Who would have guessed that our final conversation would be about lunch? From the moment of that last exchange, my memories become disjointed. A series of life-changing events took place within the space of no more than three heartbeats, and I remember them only as distinct images, like mental moments caught in a strobe light, a jagged sort of slow motion.

There was a truck. An old black pickup truck. I first noticed it when we entered a sharp curve at the top of the long hill because it suddenly appeared in our lane, speeding toward our car. Given that I was driving the speed limit, and the truck was going even faster, we were closing at a rate of at least 120 miles per hour.

It took a moment for me to realize what was happening. I remember thinking, "He's not supposed to be in my lane!" Then I ran through a split-second mental checklist of options:

- *If I swerve left to avoid him, he might realize what has happened and turn back into his lane at the same time. Then we would not only hit head-on, but in his lane. And, since we are in a blind curve, I don't know what else might be coming.*
- *If I hit the brakes and turn hard left in an attempt to get off the road regardless of what he does, our old sedan will probably roll over.*
- *Turning right is not an option, because the truck is clearly drifting across the lane in that direction.*

Since the truck was heading off the road to our right, I chose to bear gradually to the left, thinking it would certainly pass us as it ran into the ditch.

I chose wrong.

For a moment, it seemed that we had dodged the bullet. I have a momentary but clear mental image of the truck leaving the road to our right. In the corner of that picture, I see Bethany, silently, looking up.

And there the pictures run out. The next thing I recall is the sickening thud and concussive noise of an explosive impact, like being at ground zero when a bomb goes off.

The driver of the dump truck I had passed no more than twenty seconds before saw everything unfold, and described it for us later. The black pickup did run off onto the shoulder, but that jarred its drunk and sleepy driver into some measure of alertness. He instinctively pulled hard on the wheel and turned sharply back onto the road, just as I began easing our car to the left. His truck slammed into the front passenger door and ripped open the right side of our car before rolling over some fifty yards farther on. The impact brought our forward progress to an immediate stop, wrenching the car sideways and through a 360-degree loop on our way into the ditch on the opposite side of the road.

Not that I remember any of this—I was out cold from the moment of impact. But this is what I have been told.

The blackout did not last long. Before anyone else reached the car, my jangled brain began to swim its way back through a dreamlike fog, struggling toward wakefulness. Mental images of the truck lurching toward us replayed themselves over and over as I fought for consciousness. There was blinding pain, a deep red glow behind my eyes, and a debilitating sense of confusion.

I willed my eyes to open. Incredibly, my contact lenses were still in place, but nothing else was where it belonged, including my right arm, which was hanging at an awkward angle. Just past my arm, I saw mostly daylight and the twisted metal rim of what had been our right rear tire. It was smoking.

Slowly it dawned on me that I was indeed waking up, but not from sleep, not from a dream. The broken car in which I sat was all too real. The roaring din I heard was not the product of my imagination, but the sound of our car's engine still running at full tilt. Though torn away from the transmission, the engine was still running on cruise control.

I issued a mental command for my right arm to reach up and switch off the engine, but it would not obey. In fact, nothing below the shoulder would move at all. I used my left hand to pick up my right arm and put it into my lap. I remember thinking how heavy it was, just dead weight.

I reached across with my left hand and twisted the ignition key into the "off" position. The overheated engine stopped racing but started dieseling and would not shut off.

The mental exercise of dealing with the engine completed my journey toward consciousness, and I quickly became aware that something was missing. I had looked out the right side of the car and had seen only twisted metal and grass.

Bethany.

Where was Bethany?

Why wasn't she calling out or crying? Surely she would be hurt or scared.

Bethany had been in the seat beside me, but the seat was no longer where it belonged. I tried to turn around and look behind me, but was hindered by my seatbelt and a flopping right arm. In a rising panic, I unlatched the seatbelt with my left hand and worked it around my non-functional arm. Then I used my left arm to pull the right one tight across my torso so I could twist around in the seat.

Bethany was right behind me. The force of the impact had pushed her seat—with the safety belt still buckled—into the space once occupied by the back seat, near the middle of the car. The seat back was broken so that it appeared to be reclining.

Bethany lay perfectly still, with her head turned away from me, facing right. Her eyes were closed, her lips slightly parted. A bit of her tongue protruded from between clenched teeth. It was blue.

Perhaps it was that small blue tip of her tongue that told me she was dead, that my parental nightmare had come true. I reached for Bethany with my left hand, straining unsuccessfully to twist further in the seat, unaware that my movement was impeded by a long string of broken and displaced ribs in the right side of my back.

I touched the right side of Bethany's neck with trembling fingers, feeling for a pulse that was no longer there. I tried the other side of her neck, but there was nothing. Bethany remained still, unmoving, unaffected by my panicked prodding.

A swelling cry filled my lungs and erupted in a moaning shout. "Oh God!" I cried. "Bethany!" And again, "Oh God! Bethany!" And again, *"Oh God! Bethany!"* And again. And again. And again.

The driver from the dump truck had reached the car by that time. Through foggy eyes, I saw him peer into the cavity that had been the car's right side. He took one look at Bethany, seeing facial damage that was hidden from me, and a stricken expression came over his face. He began to pray aloud in a faltering voice. "Oh dear Jesus," he prayed. "Oh dear Jesus, please take this child unto yourself and hold her close. Oh dear Jesus . . . ." I cannot recall the exact words, but it was along those lines. He continued to pray in that sincere, broken voice, as if he were offering some sort of last rites, but all I remember for certain is "Oh dear Jesus" and "take this child."

I guess I was praying, too, though all I could say was "Oh God! Bethany!"

A man opened the driver's side door. I don't know if it was the truck driver or someone else. He asked if I could walk and insisted that I should get out of the car. Whether he was afraid the gas tank might explode, or thought I needed to lie down, or judged that it would be good to distance me from Bethany, I don't know. I didn't want to leave Bethany's side, but felt powerless to resist someone who appeared to know what he was doing. My legs were wobbly, but they worked, and I allowed him to lead me to the front of the car and help me down onto the deep roadside grass. On the way, I caught a momentary glimpse of the black truck, some fifty yards further down the road. It was upside down.

The man retrieved my bright blue ski jacket from the car and spread it over me. It brought little comfort or warmth, however, as I lay restlessly on the cold ground and fought for breath and continued to cry, "Oh God! Bethany!" No other words would come.

No other words seemed to matter.

Silently, I watched the man lift the hood of my car and remove the top from the air cleaner. He threw handfuls of dirt into the carburetor until the dieseling engine finally, mercifully, choked and died.

Other people began to arrive, emergency medical technicians among them. I was kept on the ground and not allowed to see what was happening with Bethany. It seemed that more people than necessary were working to stabilize me. Though I suspected that Bethany was dead, I pleaded with them to help her. I thought, however irrationally, that they might yet be able to bring her back.

I did not realize at the time that the right side of Bethany's face was badly damaged and her skull was crushed, possibly by the truck's bumper. Mercifully, I had not seen the awful result of the impact on her sweet face, which had been turned slightly away from me. Those who did see found it hard to keep their composure.

I remember brief vignettes from the ten or fifteen or twenty minutes that I spent on the ground, surrounded by activity. I remember hearing one of the first EMTs shouting for another to "Call Patrick!" so the unit there would send their ambulance. A young man, perhaps still in his teens, was assigned the task of keeping me on the ground and monitoring my condition. I pressed him again and again to tell me for sure if Bethany was dead. He didn't want to do it. Perhaps he had been instructed not to say anything, but his eyes told the story. Finally, he nodded his head. He tried to put it in words that were choked, and I do not remember them. He was trying not to cry, but his eyes were wet.

Staring into the sun-washed January sky, I began to pelt myself with self-recrimination. The dream-like state of having been unconscious and the growing symptoms of shock left me wondering if I had fallen asleep and caused the wreck. "Bethany is dead," I thought, "and it's my fault."

I mentally replayed the moments leading up to the wreck again and again, but there was a temporary gap in my memory. I conjectured that I might have gone to sleep and drifted into the left lane, waking up only when the other driver swerved to avoid me. It was a horrifying thought. What if the wreck was all my doing? I couldn't imagine having to face Jan with the knowledge that I was responsible for killing our daughter and perhaps even the driver of the other vehicle.

The more I thought about it, the more fearful I became that it was my fault, that I had caused the wreck, that Bethany was dead and I was to blame. The thought became obsessive.

Thus, when I saw the "Smoky Bear" hat of a state trooper silhouetted against the pale blue sky, I feared the worst. But then the officer leaned down and told me that the driver of the pickup appeared to be intoxicated. The skid marks and the reports of an eyewitness made it obvious that the other driver had crossed the centerline and caused the wreck. Relief washed over me in such tangible waves that I felt guilty for tasting the joy of it. "It wasn't my fault!" cried the voice that was working overtime inside my head. *"It wasn't my fault!"*

What comfort I found quickly evaporated when I heard the unmistakable clicking of a camera shutter. An ambulance-chasing, self-styled "legal aid" had arrived. I learned later that he monitored a police scanner and made a practice of rushing to accidents and photographing the crash scenes in all their graphic glory. He then offered to sell the photos to lawyers for use as evidence if a trial or lawsuit ensued.

I didn't know all that at the time, but I knew someone was taking pictures of Bethany's broken and bleeding body. I felt in my gut that it was a terrible invasion of her privacy, and I was helpless to protect her from the indignity of it.

I tried to get up and go after him, but the paramedics kept me down. I cried out for the photographer to stop. I pleaded for him to identify himself, to come talk to me and tell me what he was doing. He refused to answer me or to stop taking pictures. I never saw his face, but he later sold his pictures to the prosecuting attorneys. We did not ask to see them.

After the emergency personnel loaded me onto a stretcher and into the back of an ambulance, my thoughts were drawn away from Bethany as we drove from the scene and as the paramedics peppered me with questions about my own condition. I became aware of an intense, searing pain on the right side of my back and in my right arm. There was a growing sense of pressure on my lungs, and I found it increasingly difficult to breathe. The technicians gave me oxygen and worked to start IV fluids, but the bumpy road made the task difficult. Finally, the driver pulled over and stopped the ambulance long enough for the med tech to get the IV inserted and dripping, then sped on down the curving road.

I grunted in pain with every bump, wandering deeper into the fuzzy world of mental and physical shock. Certain that my back or arm would need surgery, I prayed to reach the hospital, go under the anesthesia, and be put out of my misery.

✳

Jan

The winter morning of Tuesday, January 18, 1994, came cold and dreary with overcast skies, but I was happily anticipating Bethany's return after her week with her grandparents in Lincolnton, Georgia. I was making preparations to go to the church office at Woodhaven Baptist Church where I served as minister of education and youth and Tony served as senior minister.

The phone rang at 8:20 AM. It was Tony, just wanting me to know that he and Bethany were getting ready to leave his parents' house to begin the five and one-half hour drive home. He assured me that they would arrive at the church later in the afternoon, in time for our weekly staff meeting.

Before the conversation ended, Tony said Bethany wanted to talk to me. She greeted me with "Hey, Mommy, we're getting ready to leave. We'll be home soon and I can't wait to tell you about my week with Mama Hollie and Daddy Bill. I've missed you. I love you, Mommy." I responded with "I love you, too, Bethany, and I'll see you this afternoon. Good-bye." I hung up the phone and went to the church office. Little did I know that would be the last time I would hear my precious daughter's voice.

I spent the morning at the church office. I was serving on the Youth Conference Planning Team, a group of North Carolina Baptist youth ministers, lay leaders, and pastors who were responsible for planning the program for four statewide summer youth conferences. I had been assigned to write a Bible study and was spending the morning working on the task. I took a break around noon and went home to eat lunch. I then returned to the church and continued working on the writing project.

Around 1:00 PM, the church secretary, Debbie Huskey, came and stood in the doorway of my office. She asked me if I knew when Gene Moore, the minister of music and children, would be coming into the office, or if I knew his home phone number. Gene had only been on staff at Woodhaven for a little more than two weeks. He worked part-time, and I did not know his daily schedule. I didn't think to inquire as to what Debbie needed. When she left my office, I remembered thinking that she looked worried or upset. I returned to working on my computer and the tasks I was attempting to complete that day.

About thirty minutes later, Gene and Jim Stephens (vice-chair of the deacons and a personal friend) came and stood in the doorway of the youth room. I greeted them cheerfully as I pushed my chair away from the computer. The look on both of their faces told me something was terribly wrong. They started walking toward me and then began pulling up chairs to sit down beside me. I stood up as Gene began speaking. He said, "Jan, there has been an accident. Tony has some broken bones and other injuries, and they think he is going to be okay . . . but your daughter Bethany . . . she . . ."

Gene didn't have to finish the sentence. I began screaming and tried to run around Gene and Jim to get out of the room. Jim grabbed me and pulled me tightly into his arms as I dropped to the floor. He fell to his knees with me and enveloped me in his arms. He held me as I yelled, "Oh God, no, not Bethany! Oh, God, no, not my child! She's the only child we have! No! No! No!" With my head buried in Jim's chest I just screamed, "No! No!" over and over in utter disbelief that my only child could be dead.

Jim soon got me seated in a chair. My body went numb, and my heart was racing. I felt a sickening queasiness in my stomach. My mind did not want to believe the news I had just heard. I told Jim I thought I was going to be sick. For the next hour I sat in a chair, leaning over a trash can as waves of nausea came over me. I remember many church members arriving and offering hugs and words of comfort, even as I held my head over the trash can. I would occasionally raise my head and look around the room. I saw the faces of shocked friends staring back at me with a deep sadness in their eyes. Someone would occasionally sit in front of me and hold my hands. Others would pray with me. Gene and Debbie began making phone calls to inform church members and friends of the news about the wreck, Tony's injuries, and Bethany's death.

The physical distress soon gave way to a sense of needing to do something. I realized that I needed to call my immediate family members. I needed to call my mother, my brother, and Tony's parents. These were phone calls I did not want to make. I first called my brother, Ben. My sister-in-law Carole answered the phone. With a trembling voice I told her that there had been a wreck and that Bethany had been killed. She just said, "Oh, God, no!" and gave the phone to my brother. I told Ben what had happened and asked him to go and share the news with our mother. After he shared the news with her, they came to the church to be with me.

While I was making these necessary phone calls, Gene was gathering information from Byerly Hospital in Hartsville, South Carolina, regarding Tony's injuries. He soon told me he had learned there was a good possibility that a drunk driver had caused the wreck. Gene also told me about the injuries Tony had sustained. I wanted to go and be with Tony, but I did not think I could make the trip to South Carolina. I explained this to my brother and asked him to go instead. My grief was so great for Bethany that I didn't feel physically or emotionally able to make the journey at the time.

My brother Ben and church members Hal Melton, Dick and Cheryl Cruickshank, Bob and Pat Barker, and Jim Stephens soon left to go to the hospital in South Carolina to be with Tony. I knew I had to begin making arrangements to get Tony home. Liz Lay (now Liz Newlin), a Woodhaven church member and a trauma nurse at Wake Medical Center, had arrived at the church. Liz offered to coordinate the plans to get Tony airlifted home the next day.

I then tried to call Tony's parents, Mama Hollie and Daddy Bill. They were not at home. I called Craig Williamson, then pastor of their church, and asked him to find Don, Tony's brother, and inform him of the wreck. Craig and Don then went to Mama Hollie and Daddy Bill's home and waited for their return to share the horrible news. Tony's parents and his brothers Jeff and Don then traveled to the hospital in Hartsville, South Carolina, to be with Tony.

Gene informed me that a nurse from Byerly Hospital had called and needed to know what funeral home we wanted to handle the arrangements for Bethany's funeral. Without giving it much thought, I told him to call Brown-Wynne Funeral Home in Cary. I don't know why I chose that funeral home. It was the only one that came to my mind at the time. Gene told me he would call the funeral home, as they would need to travel to South Carolina that evening to bring Bethany home. It broke my heart to think that she would be traveling home alone in a body bag in the back of a funeral home hearse.

Gene also tried to get in touch with Tony's son Russ, who was living with his mother in Tarboro, North Carolina. Gene reached Russ's mom and stepfather at the school where they worked and shared the news with them. Russ was a seventeen-year-old junior in high school at the time. Despite the fact that he did not live with us, he and Bethany shared a close, loving relationship. They enjoyed spending time together, and Russ was a wonderful big brother to Bethany. Russ made plans to come and be with us once Tony arrived at the hospital in Raleigh.

I finally left the church around 4:00 PM and went to our house with Carole and my mother. Walking into the house was difficult. Everywhere I looked there were reminders of Bethany. I remember sitting on the couch and staring out the window that faced our backyard. I caught sight of the swing set that now stood empty. No longer would Bethany glide through the air on the swings or slide down the sliding board. The sandbox would no longer be home to a little girl digging for treasures. No longer would the laughter of my child fill the air as she played in our yard. No longer would the neighborhood children gather at our home to play with her. Our home already felt empty.

I was in a state of shock and disbelief. My heart ached and hurt in a way I had never felt before. I was in a daze as many people began arriving at our house. Friends began cleaning each room and organizing our kitchen for the food that would soon start arriving. Fellow ministers arrived and prayed with me. Church members came and offered their presence and comfort. The phone rang constantly, bringing calls from shocked friends expressing their sadness and offering support. The ringing phone was only a reminder to me that the call would never be from Bethany. I would never hear her sweet voice again.

Reality Dawns

Tony

I thought the ambulance ride to the emergency room at Byerly Hospital in Hartsville would never end. Breathing was becoming more difficult, and the oxygen didn't seem to be helping. My back and right arm screamed with every bump. The EMT guys were using scissors to cut all my clothes away, and I remember thinking that didn't seem necessary.

The emergency room was probably much like any other, but the first one I ever saw from the patient's perspective—flat on my back, surrounded by curtains, a view of the ceiling. I fully expected to be rushed into surgery because it was obvious to me that the upper bones in my right arm were shattered; it had already swelled to twice its normal size. I not only expected surgery, but I longed for it. I was hurting so badly—both physically and emotionally—that the thought of being put to sleep was very appealing.

I was not taken to surgery, however. The medical staff seemed to be both competent and conscientious, but I recall little of what they said or did, except that they didn't seem to be in nearly the hurry I was.

I remember them asking basic questions about my medical history, though I was more interested in giving them the church phone number so someone could call Jan. I emphasized that I wanted them to tell Debbie Huskey, our friend and church secretary, and ask her to assign Gene Moore the task of telling Jan. Gene had come to our staff only recently as part-time minister of music, but I knew he had a counseling background and trusted him to handle it as well as anyone.

I was given morphine, which I didn't like, though it dulled the pain. I have hazy (thankfully) memories of my shoulder and arm being manipulated in various ways for X-rays and a CT scan. Every position hurt, but at least it distracted me from dwelling on Bethany. She was brought to the morgue in the same hospital, but no one there ever told me.

Back in the emergency room after the scan, I recall two memorable visits. One was from Gail and Billy Hutto. Gail was Gene Moore's sister, and they just happened to live in Hartsville. Gene had called them; they came immediately to the hospital, offering to help in any way they could. As other well wishers and a few curiosity seekers began to arrive, they looked out for me, setting up shop in the waiting area to intercept unwanted company and remaining there to greet my family members and friends. I was about three hours from my home in Raleigh and three hours from my family in Georgia. It would be a while yet before anyone arrived.

The second visitor was a welcome sight. It was the state trooper who had come to me as I lay by the roadside to tell me that the other driver appeared to have been drinking. Now he brought news that his suspicions had been confirmed. A blood test at the hospital had shown a blood alcohol level of .203—well over twice the level at which one is legally "drunk." With his hat off and without the sun behind him, I saw his face for the first time—a very human face within his official uniform. There was a deep sadness in his eyes. This was not something he enjoyed doing.

I was emotionally gratified to learn with certainty that the other driver was at fault, because I had continued to be plagued with guilt for my inability to avoid the wreck. I didn't feel entirely off the hook, but at least I knew it was the other driver who had put Bethany and me in harm's way.

Eventually, I was moved to a room in the intensive care unit. A grandfatherly doctor came in and explained that my arm was indeed broken, but an orthopedist would have to be consulted before they decided what to do with it. He also told me that six ribs were broken on the right side of my back, with three of them being displaced—meaning they were not only broken completely through, but the broken ends no longer met as they should. He showed me an X-ray and I could see how the ends of the ribs now overlapped each other. Surely they would have to operate to re-align them, I thought, but he assured me that, while some European surgeons did such operations, most American doctors just left them alone. The ribs would eventually grow back together in their new configuration, with a bony knot surrounding the join.

Finally, he explained that my right lung had collapsed, perhaps punctured by the broken end of a rib, and that he would need to put a suction tube into my chest cavity to draw a vacuum and keep my lung inflated while the wound healed. He then turned to a cart containing a big needle, a scalpel, and something that had every appearance of being a clear garden hose. I'm sure there were other items on the tray, but those are the things I remember.

He chose a spot on the lower right side of my chest, about two inches above the bottom of the rib cage, and plunged the needle in to deaden the area. I wished that he had brought a bigger needle, because when he took the scalpel and began making a short but deep incision to penetrate the chest cavity between two ribs, I felt every stroke. That was minor, however, compared to the burning pain that erupted when he pressed the end of that thick tube through the incision and into my chest. It was important for the fit to be tight so it didn't leak air, and I could feel the incision stretching to make room. The surgeon attached the tube to a pump on the floor, smiled in a self-effacing way, and left me alone to ponder the new appendage I had gained—and the daughter I had lost.

Much of that first afternoon is lost in a haze of morphine and Demerol, which left me trance-like, though I remember lying in bed, picking fragments of glass from my chest and face. At some point Jan called, but there were no phones in the ICU rooms. Everyone in the ICU knew the situation we were in, however. Jan was so torn from losing Bethany and so anxious to talk with me that one of the nurses gave Jan her cell phone number so she could try reaching me on the mobile phone.

Unfortunately, cell phones were just coming into vogue in 1994. Reception was poor inside the hospital, and impossible inside my room. Eventually, the staff went to a great deal of trouble to roll my bed, pump, and IVs into the hallway, where there was a weak signal. I wanted to talk to Jan more than anything, but I also dreaded it. Drunk driver or no drunk driver, I still felt responsible for Bethany's death. She had been in my care, and I had failed to get her home safely. I was afraid that Jan, who had often critiqued my driving, would put the blame squarely on my shoulders and hold it against me for the rest of my life.

But she was not in a mood for casting blame. I told her I was sorry and explained what the trooper had told me, that a drunk driver had caused the wreck. Jan assured me that she did not blame me or hold it against me. I was so grateful for her words of grace in that dark hour, for they enabled us to move on to more important things, to the grief we shared, the nightmare every parent dreads. We wondered briefly what we would do without Bethany and realized that question could not be answered in a short phone call.

Jan explained why she wanted to stay at home rather than coming to the hospital, and though I wanted to see her desperately, I told her I understood. In many ways, she was hurting as badly as I was, and I knew she needed to be where friends could minister to her. There were others who could come and look after me.

And, late in the afternoon, several people did arrive. A carload of friends from Woodhaven came—all dear people with whom we had worked closely and shared a deep mutual appreciation.

After checking in at the hospital, they found out where my car had been towed and went to recover what was left of our luggage and other things that were in the car, including the small, leather-bound planner I used for my calendar, address book, and "to-do" list. I was surprised that they found it. While there, they also took pictures of the car, for which I was grateful. In time, I knew I would want to see them. I had only seen the damage from inside the car and would never see the actual wreckage again.

My parents arrived about the same time. Both of my brothers came, and I remember being particularly touched by that. With ICU visitation rules being what they were, I barely saw them, but they were there, and I appreciated it.

At some point, my son Russ called and I was able to speak briefly with him via the same awkward cell-phone-in-the-hallway arrangement. Russ was my son by a previous marriage. Though he did not live with us, we were very close. Both of us were anxious just to hear the other's voice.

My parents stayed in the room with me as much as the nurses would allow, and I'm sure they bent the rules out of compassion, given the circumstances. I remember little of our conversation, other than asking for more stories about what they and Bethany had done together during that joyful week in grandparent-land, a week that none of us dreamed would be her last.

Late in the evening, I remember Hal Melton asking if there was anything he could do, and I asked him to go and check on the man who had caused the wreck. Surprisingly, I felt some sense of compassion and concern for him. As irresponsible as his behavior was and as careless as his driving was, I knew he had meant us no harm. He had not set out that morning to kill a child. I could imagine the inner torment he must be experiencing as he sobered up and fully realized the awful thing he had done.

When Hal reported back, I learned that the man—we'll call him "Darrell" out of consideration for his privacy—was twenty-nine years old, and the only injury he had suffered was a bump on the head. The doctor was keeping him overnight for observation. As far as I knew, he would be arrested shortly after his release and charged with causing Bethany's death.

As the night grew long, I remained strangely numb, my brain swimming in a sea of painkillers, yet struggling to make sense of what had happened and what it might mean. I came to some realizations, if not answers, and I did not want to forget them or to keep them to myself. I wanted to share what I was thinking with our church family at Bethany's funeral, but I could not imagine being out of the hospital in time to attend, much less to speak. I knew there would be conversations in which some people would try to explain away Bethany's death as God's will, and I was determined that her funeral, at least, should include what I believed to be a more appropriate theological perspective.

So, I determined that I would write a letter to the church, expressing what I was feeling, hopeful that Jan would have someone read it at the funeral. I was flat on my back, hurting with every breath and barely able to move, but I could not rest until that letter was written. Sometime around 2:00 AM, I asked my dad to help me. He used both hands to hold my small notebook above my chest. Since I am left-handed and my left arm was uninjured, I was able to scribble as he held the little book.

I wrote what I wanted to say, and when I finished—for the first time that day—I was able to cry with more than my voice and heart. The shock and pain I had been feeling had been like a hot churning vapor that boiled through body and being. Once the letter was done, the vapor cooled just enough to condense into tears, and they became a constant companion for many days.

Here is the text of the letter:

It is important for me to say this to you. Thank you for allowing me.

Let no one say that this tragic death is the will of God, under any circumstance. Let no one think for a minute that this child's heavenly parent needed her more than her earthly parents, or that the angelic chorus needed her sweet voice more than our own children's choir.

Bethany's death is not the result of God's divine or beneficent choice. Rather, it comes as the end result of the cumulative bad choices made by a man who was also created as a child of God. He did not set out to kill our daughter, but it is his behavior—and not God's—that brings us to this place.

I do not ask why this happened, nor do I ever expect to look back and understand some hidden purpose of God in Bethany's death. There is no "why" for this tragedy—there is only a "what"—the hard reality that my precious little daughter is gone from this earth.

I have no fear for her future—Bethany's faith was as pure as the snow she longed for, and God's promises are as sure as the rising sun. Now she plays with her Grandfather Rush and Grandpa Tilley, and we are left with only her toys and the indelible memories of a childhood bright with promise, and filled with love. These memories will never die.

Bethany will live always in our hearts, and God—and you—will see us through. We will never be the same again, but we will be what we can. Be patient with us as we heal, for it may take a lifetime.

Be prayerful for us, but most of all, be careful what choices you make—for good, and not for evil.

The letter was indeed read at Bethany's funeral. In time, it was printed in a variety of publications and even translated into Spanish. I had no idea that others would find it so helpful or that it would be shared in so many ways. At the moment the important thing was simply getting it out of my heart and head and onto paper. It was the first tentative step on a long road to emotional recovery.

✳

Jan

Tuesday evening, my body was in a state of shock and I felt numb. I could not believe that Bethany was dead; I longed to wake up from what seemed to be a horrible dream. My home was filled with family, friends, and church members. I didn't know what to say to anyone. I had no words to voice the overwhelming sense of loss and pain stirring within me.

I wanted to talk to Tony. I tried to call the hospital in South Carolina several times, but the switchboard operator couldn't seem to get me connected to the intensive care unit. When I finally got through to an ICU nurse, she told me there was no phone by Tony's bed, and he was too heavily sedated to talk in any case. I pleaded with her to please make it possible for me to speak with Tony. The kind nurse finally gave me her cell phone number and told me to call back around 6:30 PM. She assured me that she would do whatever was necessary to get me connected with Tony.

I called the nurse's cell phone at the appointed time. However, the phone signal was horrible. The nurses had to roll Tony out into a hallway in order to get a decent signal. The phone was finally given to Tony, who did not make a whole lot of sense as he talked. He was drowsy and "fuzzy-headed" due to the heavy doses of drugs he was receiving for pain. He was able to tell me that the state trooper who investigated the wreck had visited with him earlier. The trooper informed Tony that the driver of the truck was drunk and had a blood alcohol content of .203. I fell to the kitchen floor and screamed, "No, don't tell me that! Oh, God, a drunk driver killed Bethany!" I remember telling Tony that we were working out the details to get him back home on a life-flight the next day. I assured Tony that I did not blame him for Bethany's death. I told him I loved him and would see him around lunchtime the next day.

I do remember going upstairs to my bedroom after the phone call. When I reached the top of the stairs, I turned to my right to look into Bethany's bedroom. I was shocked to find that someone had closed the door to her room. Why was this door shut? Who did this? Why would someone do this? Obviously, someone must have thought that since Bethany was dead, the door to her room should be shut. Perhaps they had presumed it would be too painful for me to see Bethany's room and all of her belongings. I opened the door and announced to those within hearing distance that I wanted it to remain open.

I then went to Bethany's closet. I opened the doors and stood staring at all of her Sunday dresses. I touched them with my hands. I held some of them up to my nose, trying to capture a scent of Bethany. I stared at the dresses, aware that I needed to choose one for her burial. Which dress should I choose? Which one was her favorite? Again, the reality of the situation came over me. Bethany was dead, and I needed to decide on a dress for her to wear, not to church, but for her funeral.

I moved to the chest of drawers that held Bethany's other clothing. I needed to find a slip to go with the dress. I didn't know what else to choose. Again, I asked myself: Do I need to pick out socks? Do I need to send underwear to the funeral home? What about shoes? I had never done this before, and the task proved to be unsettling and upsetting. I needed someone to help me make these decisions.

I wanted our friend and Woodhaven church member Janice Haywood to be with me during this time. She was in Kansas City, leading Vacation Bible School conferences for the Baptist Sunday School Board (now Lifeway Christian Resources). Someone from Janice's office at the Baptist

State Convention of North Carolina had already informed her of Bethany's death. Unknown to me, Janice had been trying to reach me during the late afternoon. We were finally able to speak by phone early Tuesday evening. I told her what details I had about the wreck and the extent of Tony's injuries. I also explained that we had learned a drunk driver had caused the wreck.

As I talked with Janice, I voiced the fear that I did not think I could walk through these next few days alone. She assured me I would find the strength and courage I would need for the days ahead. I knew Tony would not be able to help with funeral planning, and I was not certain he would even get to attend the service once he was transferred back to a hospital in Raleigh. I needed someone to assist me with funeral arrangements and the many details that required my attention. I felt that Janice was the person who could help me make the best decisions in the midst of the grief I was experiencing. She assured me she would do whatever she could to assist me and made arrangements to arrive home the next morning.

Sue Colenda, whom I had met in 1982 while working at Oxford Orphanage, arrived at our home later in the evening. She came with a suitcase, planning to stay as long as I needed her, to do whatever she could to give support and assistance. Her presence was a welcome comfort.

The Baptist women's group from the church had their monthly meeting that evening. Afterward, the women came to our house to visit with me. I was sitting at the dining room table when they arrived. They listened as I shared the few details I had regarding the wreck and Tony's condition. Their presence meant more than any words they could say. I remember looking at them and saying, "If you have children, please go home tonight and hug them a little tighter at bedtime and tell them you love them." Again, the reality of Bethany's death was sinking in as I realized I would never tuck her in bed again.

My mother decided to spend the night with me. We lay in the same bed that night, but sleep did not come for either one of us. Our bodies and minds were still in shock. I stared at the ceiling and tried to let my mind absorb the horrible events of this day. I tossed and turned as my thoughts turned to Tony. I knew I needed to be with him in the hospital in South Carolina, and I felt guilty for not making the trip to be there. I wanted to hold him and be held by him. I imagined he was having some of the same thoughts I was having. Why did this happen? Can Bethany really be dead? What will we do without her? What will life be like for us now?

I also thought about Bethany. When I did try to close my eyes to sleep, I imagined what the wreck must have been like for her. I wondered what she must have felt or experienced. Had she seen the truck coming? What were the last words she said to her daddy? Did she cry out at the moment of impact? Did she feel pain? Did she really die instantly?

I also blamed myself for her death. Tony and I had originally planned for one of us to go to Georgia on Sunday and return home with Bethany on Monday. Those plans changed because we both needed to attend a long-range planning meeting for the church on Sunday evening. As I lay in bed, I reasoned with myself that Bethany would not be dead had I gone to Georgia on Sunday. I went through a litany of "what ifs." What if Tony and Bethany had left his parents' home just a few minutes earlier or later? What if I had kept Bethany on the phone with me that morning for a little longer? What if I had never sent her to Georgia for nine days? What if I had been in the car with them? What if I had been driving the car?

I wondered how Tony and I would ever get through this awful time. What would life be like for us in the coming days? How would we go on? Would we survive this terrible blow to our hearts? Questions filled my mind as I thought of my precious child, but no answers came during that long, dark, and lonely night. The questions, void of any answers, lingered in my mind throughout the night.

I remember feeling a sense of panic when I realized that I did not know where Bethany was. Was she at the hospital? Was she in a cold storage locker in the morgue? I had not thought to ask anyone at the hospital where she was and could only assume that she was in the hospital morgue or in the back of a hearse making the trip to the funeral home in Cary. Wherever she was, I just wanted to be with her. I wanted to hold her in my arms. I was still awake at 5:30 AM, and the reality of Bethany's death broke with the dawn.

A Hard Way to
Say Good-bye

Tony

When I emerged from a drugged stupor long enough to realize that another morning had dawned after all, I learned that one of our church friends had taken the lead in arranging a life flight so I could be transported to the trauma unit at Wake Medical Center, closer to home. It was encouraging to learn that I would have some of the best care available, but even more heartening to know I'd be returning home, closer to Jan and our church family.

Late in the morning, the friends and family who had come to support me in Hartsville climbed into their cars and set out for three-hour drive to Raleigh. An ambulance transported me to a small airport that I remember only for the chain-link fence I could see as we drove through the gates and for the aging tarmac where a shiny white jet awaited me.

My swollen arm and broken ribs throbbed with every move, especially as the EMTs struggled to get the stretcher onto the small plane and transfer me onto the narrow bench designed for transporting patients. My broken, swollen arm hung over the side, and despite the agonizing pain, it had to be folded over my chest and strapped down for the flight. Thankfully, the life-flight nurse was Ed Sammons, whose son was involved in our church youth group. It was good to see a familiar face in such an unfamiliar setting.

I remember nothing about the journey except that the flight itself was smooth, but the experience was rough. The pilot landed gently, but the bump was enough to set off new flashes of pain, which increased with the transfer from the plane to another ambulance, through high-speed interstates and potholed streets, then from the ambulance to a gurney in the trauma room at WakeMed. The shattered bones in my arm and the broken ribs in my back ground against each other with every movement. Those and the stiff vacuum tube running through my chest wall contributed to excruciating jolts of pain with every movement.

Finally, however, I was parked in a curtained stall of the trauma room, and Jan was allowed to come in. I remember little of what was said, only that she was there, that she held my hand, and that we cried together, still asking, "What will we do without Bethany?" I still felt somewhat responsible for Bethany's death. Even though the drunken driver was clearly at fault, I felt I could have done something differently. If I had been more alert, had made better judgments, had responded more quickly, perhaps Bethany would not be dead. I told Jan I was sorry, and she assured me that she did not hold me responsible. All too soon, the trauma doctor arrived and Jan had to leave.

The next few days were a painful mix of medical tests, embarrassing but necessary bathroom procedures, and a steady stream of visitors, most of whom I was happy to see. I learned later that many more had come to the hospital—ministry colleagues, church members, and other friends. The staff in the intensive care unit finally resorted to limiting visits to family and asking visitors to sign a notepad so I would know they had come.

The restrictions did not prevent one church member from talking her way past the nurses at 2:00 AM one morning. Another sweet-talked her way in at midnight the following evening. I was honored that they wanted to see me so badly, but I probably wasn't good company.

The best thing about going into ICU was that doctors inserted an epidural line into my spine, which succeeded in controlling the pain from my ribs. The addition of Toradal to the drug regimen finally dulled the pain in my arm. With pulsing air blankets wrapped around my legs to promote circulation and a variety of other tubes attached, I couldn't have gotten out of bed if I'd wanted to.

In time, I was moved to a private room on the orthopedic floor, where visitors had greater access. This was not necessarily a good thing. I am an introvert by nature and was already under more stress than I could have previously imagined. There was a limit to how much company I could appreciate in one day.

On my second day in the orthopedic ward, a local pastor and his wife showed up at 7:00 AM and settled in for a much longer visit than I was ready for. I pretended to sleep, but still they stayed. I truly appreciated their concern, but I resolved to be more sensitive to the patient's needs when I returned to the other side of the hospital equation.

Jan came almost every day. Sadly, in her first visits, our conversations had to address funeral plans. Our close friend, Janice Haywood, had left a conference and flown halfway across the country to be with Jan. She was very helpful in accompanying her to the funeral home, choosing a casket and burial plot, and looking after other details. Those were things I simply could not do from a hospital bed. Thankfully, though, Jan encouraged me to be involved in choosing the speakers, music, and pallbearers for Bethany's funeral.

On the day of the funeral, several friends who ordinarily would have attended the service spent the time with me so I would not be alone in the hospital, and I was humbled by their gift of presence.

Later that day, Jack Glasgow came by. Jack is a longtime friend and an amazing pastor. Though he did not know Bethany well, he knew Jan and me, and we had asked him to offer the eulogy at her funeral. The service had included a recording of "A Whole New World," a beautiful song from Bethany's favorite movie, *Aladdin*. When Bethany left this world for the next one, the song took on a new meaning for us, as we imagined her exploring a whole new world.

Jack had stopped by the Disney store and bought a large snow globe with the characters from *Aladdin* inside. A wind-up music box in the bottom played the melody of "A Whole New World." I kept the globe in the bed with me for days, cradling its smooth surface, occasionally winding up the music box and crying like a baby.

Almost daily, it seemed, my bed would be rolled through the halls and down the elevator to an X-ray lab, then lined up against a wall with others who were awaiting X-rays. I grew to dread the orderly's approach. The added movement always raised the pain level, and there was an emotional toll. I appreciated the orderly's good cheer but could not share it. It felt awkward to be parked beside other patients while we waited. I did not feel like talking to them, and I suspect they were lost in their own pain and didn't feel like talking to me. I tended to lay in silence, staring at the ceiling, fighting back tears.

Early mornings, however, were the most difficult. I encouraged Jan to stay home at night and rest as much as she could because her days were both physically and emotionally exhausting. For me, hospital days were busy, generally including a string of visitors to entertain (most of them welcome), punctuated by catheterizations, one-handed meals, and trips to the

X-ray lab. At night I was given enough medication to fall asleep, but it would last only until 5:30 or 6:00 AM, when I would wake up to a dark and empty room. In those quiet hours I felt desperately alone, almost lost. Our friend Janice asked one day if there was anything she could do for me, and I told her what I wanted most was a friendly face about 6:00 AM the next morning. She showed up to keep me company and listen to my pain, and I have never forgotten it.

In time, the big vacuum tube was yanked from my side with little more ceremony or gentleness than had accompanied its insertion. The epidural catheter controlling the pain from my fractured ribs was removed, which brought a new dimension to my feeble attempts at moving about the bed. Finally, sufficient wires and tubes were unplugged to allow me to stand, with assistance, and to gingerly walk around the room. For two days, I was sent on hiking excursions down the hall and back.

On the seventh day, they sent me home.

Being untethered and coming home was a bit frightening, but also exciting. It was easier to visit with family and friends, for which I was grateful—though it was also more difficult to dissuade those who stayed too long.

Ben Rush, my brother-in-law, brought over a new recliner for me to use, and it was as comfortable as anything could be at the time. The doctors suggested that I sleep on a big foam wedge to elevate my upper body, and a friend provided one she had used. Friends, church members, and neighbors continued to bring far more food than we could eat.

A couple of days after my return, I felt strong enough to watch a videotape of Bethany's funeral. Knowing that the experience would be a trial for Jan as well as for me, several friends came over to watch it with us and offer their support. Afterward, they shared favorite memories of Bethany. We cried, but we also smiled, and I was grateful.

*

Jan

On Wednesday, the day after Bethany died, Tony was scheduled to return by life-flight, arriving at the Raleigh-Durham airport around 11:30 AM. A friend from Woodhaven took me and other family members to the hospital. When we arrived, we were directed to a family waiting area near the emergency room. Our friend Liz finally came out and informed me that I could see Tony for a few minutes. I followed her to a small cubicle. Liz showed me in, pulled the curtain shut, and left me alone with Tony.

I gently hugged Tony, sat down beside his bed, and held his left hand as we wept together. Tony tried to explain that he did everything he could to avoid the wreck, but he still felt responsible. He said, "I'm so sorry I killed our daughter." Through my tears I told Tony I did not blame him. I assured him that Bethany was dead because of a drunk driver. I felt very helpless as I sat by Tony, knowing that he was in great pain and feeling tremendous guilt and grief. His hands, arms, and chest were still full of shattered glass. His right arm hung limply beside him, and a tube emerged from the right side of his chest, attached to a vacuum pump that kept his right lung inflated. He was physically and emotionally broken.

The head trauma doctor and a resident orthopedist soon came in to begin assessing Tony's injuries and informed me I would have to leave. They told me I would be able to see Tony again after he was moved to the intensive care unit. Tony and I talked briefly about funeral arrangements, as I was to go to the funeral home once I left the hospital. We talked about speakers for the funeral service and musical selections. Tony suggested that we use the Scripture "Let the little children come to me, for such is the kingdom of God" (Mark 10:14). I told Tony I would see him later that night, kissed him good-bye, and returned to the emergency room waiting area.

The waiting area was filled with family members, friends, and several area ministers. I fell into the arms of my sister-in-law, Carole, and she held me as I cried. My mother was also there with us, and Mama Hollie and Daddy Bill arrived soon. Mama Hollie held me as I cried out, "What are we going to do without Bethany? What are we going to do?"

Jack Glasgow, pastor of Zebulon Baptist Church, sat in front of me and held my hands as I continued crying out in disbelief and shock. I told him Tony and I had talked briefly about the funeral and wanted him to have a part in the service. I spoke through tears as I told him some of what we had discussed. Jack just held me and let me cry. All I could say was "What are we going to do without Bethany? What are we going to do? How will we go on without her?"

Janice had come straight to the hospital upon returning from Kansas City. I asked her to go to the funeral home with me. My friend Sue also went with us. Upon arriving at the funeral home, the three of us sat with the funeral director and began the task of making many decisions. I had never been the one in charge of making funeral arrangements for someone. I was familiar with the process through previous personal grief experiences and with those I had ministered to as a church staff member, but none of those experiences had prepared me for planning a funeral for my child.

After giving the funeral director all the necessary information for the obituary, reviewing the price list of available services, and filling out the necessary paperwork, I was told it was time to choose a casket. The funeral director explained that I needed to choose an "adult-sized" casket for Bethany, as she was a few inches too tall to fit into a child's casket.

Janice, Sue, and I were then directed to the casket showroom, which proved to be overwhelming. I thought to myself, "This is not really happening to me. This has to be a very bad dream and I need to wake up now." I did not want to believe I had to choose a casket for my daughter.

The funeral home director showed us where the cost for each casket was displayed, and then he left the room. We walked around the room for a while, looking at all the caskets. I was wishing that Tony had been there to help me with the decision. I walked by bronze and silver caskets, along with wooden ones made of cherry or pine. Some were elaborate and some were simple. Each casket contained a small card that had the cost typed on it. Most of the caskets did not look appropriate for a seven-year-old child. I kept searching around the room, wanting to find just the right one for my Bethany. I finally ended up in a far back corner of the room and placed my hand on an oak casket. It was lined with a soft pink fabric. I looked at Janice and Sue and said, "This is the one for Bethany."

We called the funeral home director back into the room, and he informed me that I now had to choose a vault. There were three choices available, and I had no idea which one to choose. This decision was more unsettling to me than having to choose the casket, as the funeral home director began explaining how the vault would protect the casket and the body of the loved one from the elements of nature. The cost for each vault was based on the number of years of protection it should provide. After discussing the pros and cons of each vault with Janice and Sue, I finally made a decision. The reality that Bethany's body would be put in a casket, then sealed in a vault, and covered with dirt was very unsettling to me. I did not want to put her body in the ground.

My stepson Russ arrived at our home later in the afternoon. He hugged me and simply said, "I am here. I want to do whatever you need me to do over the next few days. I know that dad will not be able to be with you and I'll do what I can to help." Russ exhibited maturity far beyond his seventeen years over the next few days. I knew his heart was hurting, but he gave of himself so unselfishly with his presence and support.

Bethany's special friend, Christopher, came to the house to see me early that evening. He hugged me and told me he was sorry that Bethany had died. He shared with me what a special friend Bethany had been to him. He then presented me with a small gift box. Inside was a gold, heart-shaped necklace. As I held it in my hands, Christopher said, "I picked it out myself. If it's okay with you and Mr. Tony, I would like for you to put it around Bethany's neck and let her be buried with it." With tears streaming down my face, I said, "Christopher, I know Bethany would love this gift. You were her special friend and she loved you very much." I agreed to his precious request.

I went to the hospital to visit Tony later in the evening. The doctor came in while I was there. When I asked him if Tony would be released from the hospital by Friday so that he could attend the funeral, he looked at me sadly and said Tony would be in the hospital for at least another week. He would not be able to attend the funeral home visitation or the funeral. I realized then that I would be attending our daughter's funeral without Tony. He would not be able to have that time of closure. It was difficult news to hear. We made the decision to ask someone to videotape the funeral service so that Tony would be able to watch it once he returned home from the hospital.

We then turned to the task of making other decisions regarding Bethany's funeral service. We wanted the church pianist, Jane McNeill, to provide the musical selections. We asked Hal Melton to give a personal eulogy for Bethany. Jack Glasgow would offer words of comfort and hope from the Scriptures. Janice would lead a time of remembering Bethany with the children who attended the funeral. The congregation would join their voices in singing "Share His Love" because Bethany, in her seven short years, had taught us much about sharing the love of God with others. We chose to use the song "A Whole New World" from Bethany's favorite movie, *Aladdin*. We also chose the song "What a Wonderful World" by Louis Armstrong for the benediction. This was a special song that Bethany's second grade class had sung during a class program Tony and I attended in early December 1993. We selected four women and four men who had touched Bethany's life in special ways to serve as pallbearers.

On Thursday morning I went to the cemetery in Fuquay-Varina to pick out burial plots at Greenlawn Memorial Gardens. We had made no prior arrangements regarding our own burials, much less that of our daughter. Janice again went with me to assist in this task. Bob and Pat Barker and the owner of the cemetery met us there. This was another decision I had to make without Tony's presence or input. After walking around the cemetery for a while, I chose a spot near some beautiful magnolia trees as the final resting place for Bethany's body.

Once we left the cemetery, we went to the hospital to visit Tony and to finalize the funeral arrangements. Janice, Hal, and Jack listened as Tony and I shared our thoughts about what to include in the service. We wanted the service to be a time of worship and celebration of Bethany's life.

Later in the afternoon, I wanted to go the funeral home to view Bethany's body. I had asked the funeral home director and my own family members when I would be able to see her. No one seemed to have an answer for me. My questions and inquiries were met with only silence and sad looks.

I had already picked out Bethany's burial clothes and given them to the funeral home director. I could not understand the delay in getting her body ready. The visitation was scheduled for that same evening, and I was anxious to view her body that afternoon. Janice finally took me aside and explained the reason for the delay.

She described Bethany's injuries and told me the funeral home was having a hard time getting her face and hair fixed to look "normal." Her body had been taken to a funeral home in Raleigh so that the injuries to her face and head could be "fixed."

Janice went on to explain that the right side of Bethany's face had taken the brunt of the impact from the wreck. She told me that the funeral home employees were doing the best they could and my sister-in-law Carole was at the funeral home with them, trying to help. Carole had taken a recent photograph of Bethany with her so the morticians would know what Bethany looked like before the wreck.

No one had told me the specifics of Bethany's injuries before that moment, and I had not inquired about the full extent of them. All I had been told was that she died instantly of a basal skull fracture. Tony had told me that he had not seen any obvious injuries to Bethany's face when he looked at her immediately after the wreck. The damaged right side of her face had been turned away from him.

We finally left to go to the funeral home around 4:00 PM. Carole met me in the lobby and told me that Bethany was not going to look like herself. She and Janice tried to prepare me for what I was about to see, and

Carole held me by the arm as walked down the long aisle in the chapel. I could see Bethany's body lying in the casket as we approached.

When I finally saw her up close, I held on to the side of the casket and wept. I cried out, "Oh my God! Oh, Bethany!" Though Janice and Carole had tried to prepare me, I was still shocked to see that Bethany's right cheek was covered with makeup. I touched her cheek, and when I pulled my hand away, wet makeup was on my fingers. Hair had been removed from the back of her head to replace what had been pulled out in the forehead area. There was damage to her mouth and teeth. Bruises on her arms were covered with makeup. In my shocked state, I announced that I wanted to close the casket for the funeral home visitation. I wanted only our closest family members to be able to see her, and then I wanted the casket closed. I did not want Bethany's friends or anyone else to see what the wreck had done to her beautiful face and body.

But I knew that our family, friends, and church members would need to see her body, especially the children and the youth. I said to those in the room, "I don't want to leave the casket open, but I know that others need to see her body." Seeing her body would help them deal with the reality of her death. I wanted to keep the casket open, but only if we could keep visitors from getting close enough to see the extent of Bethany's injuries. Janice suggested we use the floral arrangements that were already in the room to form a semicircle in front of Bethany's casket so that those visiting could still see her from a distance of about ten feet. Janice and another friend would stand on either side of the flowers to ensure that visitors would not get too close to the casket. We would place a favorite photograph of Bethany on the lower part of the casket. This decision eased my mind about leaving the casket open, but it did nothing to erase the horror of seeing my child's injured body.

Before I left the funeral home, I put Christopher's gift to Bethany around her neck. The heart-shaped necklace was a beautiful reminder of the special friendship they shared.

Following dinner, we arrived back at the funeral home around 6:30 PM. My stepson Russ stood by my side the entire time. He reminded me to sit down every few minutes to rest. He kept a glass filled with water and offered it to me throughout the evening. He had tissues ready when I needed to wipe my tears. He greeted every person who came through the receiving line. I drew much strength from Russ's care and presence with me.

The last person came through the line sometime after 10:00 PM. It was a long evening, but I was surrounded by friends and family who knew and loved Bethany. I felt a tremendous outpouring of love and support. Children, youth, and adults came to express their sympathy and shared many wonderful stories and memories of Bethany. I didn't cry much during the visitation. I felt as though I was in a fog and merely going through the motions of what I had to do to get through the evening. I also wanted to speak with every person who came through the receiving line. I especially wanted to speak to the children and youth who came and to thank each of them for being a friend to Bethany.

Once visitors had left the funeral home, I asked my family and friends who were still present to wait in the lobby so I could be alone with Bethany for a few minutes. I could not leave her without saying a final good-bye. Once the doors to the chapel were closed, I knelt beside the casket and held Bethany's hand. I cried as I had my last conversation with Bethany. This is what I told her: "Bethany, you are a special daughter. Your mommy and daddy love you so very much. I have always been proud of you. I will miss you so much. I will miss holding you. I will miss rubbing your tummy at night as you fall asleep. I will miss helping you with homework. I will miss hearing you laugh. I will miss your silly knock-knock jokes. I will miss seeing you play with your friends Christopher and Molly. You were such a good friend to them and many others. You were a great little sister to Russ. I'm so sorry that mommy and daddy were unable to protect you from this. Your daddy loves you and he wanted more than anything to be with us right now. I love you, Bethany, and I will miss you. I will look forward to the day when you greet me with a big hug in heaven."

Before I left Bethany, I did what I think any mother would have done. I had to know if she had received any other injuries. I lifted the drape of material that covered the lower half of her body. The bruises on her legs were covered with make-up. Her feet were covered with the white lace socks I had chosen. I replaced the material, but what I wanted to do was take Bethany out of the casket and hold her in my arms. Since I couldn't do that, I kissed Bethany and told her I loved her. I said good-bye and walked out of the chapel. I asked the funeral home director to close the casket and not open it again. I fell into the arms of my brother, and he held me as I sobbed.

I finally was able to get sleep that night, though not without the help of some medication prescribed by a doctor. I had not slept much at all since receiving the news of Bethany's death on Tuesday. I was extremely tired, but I found it hard to close my eyes and sleep at night. My mind would not shut down. I was consumed with grief. I was worried about Tony. There were too many decisions to make. The medicine finally brought relief and rest.

I woke up on Friday morning to the realization that it was the day I would have to bury Bethany. I couldn't stand the thought of putting her in the cold ground and leaving her there alone. It was a cold and dreary January day, and I did not want to face it. Tony was not with me and I did not want to get out of bed and do what no parent should ever have to do.

There were friends in the kitchen taking care of all the meal preparations. There were friends answering the phone and taking messages for me. Others were making the beds and straightening up the house. There were faithful members at the church making final preparations for the funeral service.

I remain grateful for the many friends, family members, and church members who were so gracious in offering support and care during those days. Even so, I found myself periodically retreating to my bedroom and shutting the door. I felt emotionally drained and in need of time alone, physically exhausted from lack of sleep. I had been making trips each day to be with Tony in the hospital. I was hurting. I was feeling waves of anger toward the person responsible for the wreck. I was searching for answers to the many questions I had regarding Bethany's death, but there were no answers—only the shocking reality that Bethany was dead.

At lunchtime, I was sitting at our table with a plate of food in front of me. I did not want anything to eat. Why should I eat? Bethany would never eat another meal. Each time I sat at the table I was reminded that there would always be an empty chair. Bethany would never sit at this table again and share a meal with her family. Never again would I hear her sing her favorite blessing— *"Oh, the Lord's been good to me, and so I thank the Lord; for giving me the things I need, the sun and the moon and the apple seed."*

I looked up from my plate and focused on the picture adorning our pantry door. It was a drawing Bethany had made at school. On one side of the page was a self-portrait: she had drawn herself and titled it "This is me at 7." On the other side she had drawn an old, wrinkled version of herself with the title, "This is me at 83."

As I stared at the picture, I was struck by the reality that Bethany would never live to be eighty-three. She would not even get to be an eight-year-old little girl. She would always be seven. A wave of emotion came over me. Tears ran down my face as I excused myself from the table and the room. I ran up the stairs to our bedroom, shut the door, and fell on the floor by the bed. I stayed there for a while and wept from the depths of my aching heart. The deep sadness I had been feeling was finally released.

My friends and family left me alone for a while as I cried. They sensed that I did not need anyone to tell me to stop crying or to be strong. I did not want to hear empty explanations of why Bethany had died. I just wanted to grieve her death. I knew I would probably not let myself cry at the church during the funeral. This private time and the release of all the bottled up pain was necessary for me to be able to go to the church and get through the funeral service.

Sue and Janice later came into the bedroom and listened as I shared with them all that I had bottled up for the last few days. They gave me space and time to talk. They did not presume to know the depth of my grief, nor did they try to explain it away. Their presence and support were all I needed in that moment. Once I had finished talking, they left me alone so I could make my final preparations for the funeral service.

I found solace in music. I played a tape recording of Bethany's favorite song, "A Whole New World." The song took on new meaning for me as I thought about Bethany in heaven, in a whole new world. I was also aware that Tony and I had been thrust into a whole new world . . . a world of life without Bethany. I could not even begin to imagine what the days ahead would hold for us as we faced life without our precious daughter.

I finally began to get myself ready for the funeral. I stood in my closet just staring at my clothes and asking myself, "What does a mother wear to her daughter's funeral?" I chose an outfit that Bethany had especially liked. After dressing, I emerged from the solitude of my bedroom and returned to the land of the living. Family members from out of town had gathered in our den, patiently waiting to see me. I greeted each one of them with a hug and thanked them for their presence. They looked at me with sad eyes and offered comforting words. Soon enough, it was time to go to the church for the funeral service.

My family and I arrived at the church a few minutes before 2:00 PM. We stood in the lobby outside the sanctuary. The first faces I saw were those of the youth of the church as they were seated in the choir loft. I then saw the casket positioned in front of the pulpit. We entered the sanctuary as the pianist played a beautiful arrangement of "Jesus Loves Me." I felt totally numb as I was directed to my seat on the front row. My brother Ben was seated on one side of me, and Russ was on the other side. The church was filled to capacity with friends and family. Bethany's closed casket was directly in front of me, just a few feet away. An 8"x10" photograph of

Bethany was sitting on the casket, along with a beautiful spray of spring flowers that had lovingly been arranged by our friend Alison Bailey. The pallbearers were seated to my right. My family surrounded me, yet I felt so alone. Tony was not there to share the time with me. It wasn't right for him not to be there. I thought of him and knew how hard it must have been for him to be in the hospital at that moment.

Tony and I wanted the funeral service to be a time of both remembrance and worship. Hal led a time of remembering Bethany, sharing wonderful stories of how she laughed, how she loved, and how she touched our lives. Jack focused on the Scripture verse "Let the little children come to me, for such is the kingdom of God" (Mark 10:14). He also read the poignant message Tony had written while in the intensive care unit in South Carolina.

Janice led a time with the children. She invited all the children present to sit with her at the front of the church. She shared with them memories of Bethany and then read a letter Bethany's friend Molly Keel had written, recalling special memories of their friendship. Janice asked the children to share some of their special memories of Bethany, and then invited them and the congregation to sing along with Bethany's favorite song, "A Whole New World." I think I was the only one who was able to sing along through the whole song. Bethany and I would sing the song together while riding in the car. She would sing Jasmine's part and I would sing Aladdin's part. On the day of her funeral, I sang solo. I missed hearing her sing so strongly and sweetly.

The service concluded with the song "What a Wonderful World," by Louis Armstrong. Bethany's second grade class had used the song during a program Tony and I attended at her school in early December 1993. They had illustrated a book about China with the words to this song included. During the program, the children had taken turns reading from the book. Bethany had been responsible for the artwork on the page with the words "They're really saying 'I love you.'" After reading the book, the children sang "What a Wonderful World," imitating Armstrong's gravelly voice on the final "Oh, yeah!"

We thought it fitting to use the song at the conclusion of Bethany's funeral. She did think the world was wonderful. But all I could think about while the song played was that Bethany would never again see trees of green or red roses bloom. She would no longer be able to look at skies of blue and clouds of white. She would never see another rainbow. I would never again hear her say, "I love you, Mommy." I would not get to see my baby grow up. She was in a whole new world, and so was I. At this moment, the world did not seem so wonderful to me.

The hearse was parked in front of the main door to the sanctuary. As my family and I exited the church, I saw the casket being placed in the hearse. I wanted to crawl in and ride with my Bethany to the cemetery. I did not want her to be alone. I did not want to put her in the cold, hard ground. I was already dreading the moment when I would have to leave her at the grave.

I was directed to my seat in the family car. Holding the large photo of Bethany on my lap, I sat and watched the door of the church as hundreds of friends made their way out into the cold.

The funeral procession finally began the drive to the cemetery. I had asked that we take the road that went past Sunset Lake. It was a favorite place where Bethany and I went occasionally to walk around the lake and to sit on the deck of the clubhouse overlooking the lake. She especially liked to watch the water spill over the dam. One of my favorite pictures of her is one I took on the porch of the clubhouse. She is sitting in a white wicker chair wearing a pink and white outfit, and there is a beautiful smile on her face. It seemed appropriate that Bethany's last ride include a drive by this special place.

We arrived at the cemetery and waited in the family car as the casket was unloaded from the hearse. I watched the pallbearers walk in front of me with the casket, moving slowly up the sidewalk to the burial plot. I was led to my seat on the front row of chairs. The words Jack and Hal spoke were lost to me as I sat and stared at the casket. I could only think about Bethany's body going into the ground once the graveside service was over. I didn't want to put my child's body in the ground in this wooden box. All of my hopes and dreams for her would also be buried.

Following the graveside service, Hal and Jack hugged me, and I thanked them for their presence and support to my family. It was time to get up and leave. When Ben and Russ helped me out of my seat, I went straight to the casket and touched it. I rubbed my hand over it and said, "I don't want to leave her here." Russ and Ben cradled me in their arms and led me away from the gravesite. In my mind I knew Bethany was no longer in that body. It was a mere shell. She was home, cradled in the arms of our loving Lord and Savior, Jesus Christ. But in my heart, I wanted nothing more than to hold her in my arms and take her home with me.

As I made my way down the sidewalk away from the grave, many loving and supportive friends embraced me. I felt a tremendous outpouring of love and support from those who came to the funeral and burial. They did not have to speak any words—there was nothing they could say that could take the pain away. Their presence spoke volumes to me and brought great strength and comfort to my broken heart.

I cried few tears during the funeral. I had said my good-bye to Bethany following the funeral home visitation and had experienced a great release of emotion at home hours before the funeral service was held. I consciously held back the tears during the funeral because I am somewhat private when it comes to sharing my feelings and emotions. At that time in my life, it was rare for me to cry in public. I felt safe crying alone or with trusted friends and family members, but I had a fear of breaking down at the church in front of a crowd of people. I did not want my grief to become a public spectacle, even though I knew it would have been a normal and accepted expression of the great loss I had experienced.

I also felt a tremendous sense of responsibility to the Woodhaven family of faith. Tony was not present as their senior minister. I was serving as minister of youth and education and felt that I needed to continue in the role of minister, even then. The church family was grieving, and I felt I needed to help them with the grief they were also experiencing. For good or ill, I was unable to step out of the ministerial role.

In some ways, I surprised myself as I made my way through these first few days of grief. I discovered a strength I had not previously known or experienced. I had to make hard decisions and do difficult things I had never done before. Even so, I was aware that I needed to let others minister to me through those awful days. I did my best to find some balance between spending the necessary time I needed to be alone and being with those who wanted to offer some measure of comfort. I was also able to step out of my own pain and minister to others. The balance of filling my own needs and meeting the needs of others was important to me as a person and as a minister.

As we returned home following the burial, the house was filled with activity. A busy kitchen crew was preparing dinner for my family. A group of friends from my college days sat and listened as I shared stories about Bethany. Later in the evening, my friend Robin accompanied me to see Tony in the hospital. I sat at his bedside, held his hand, and shared with him all the details about the funeral and the burial.

On the way home, my mind was a jumble of rampaging thoughts, filled with questions. How would we go on without Bethany? What would our lives be like? Would Tony recover from his injuries soon? Would I be okay? How would we get through this? How long would our hearts hurt? Would I ever feel "normal" again? When would we be able to return to work? *Would* we be able? What was Bethany experiencing in heaven? Was she okay? With all of those thoughts swirling through my head, I made my way home through the traffic and the darkness.

And then, it happened. As we turned into our subdivision, I was greeted with a gift from heaven. Directly over our subdivision sports field, a shooting star fell from the dark sky. It took my breath away for a moment. I cried out to Robin, "Did you see that? It's from Bethany! She's throwing down stars to let me know that she is there and she's okay!" My tears dissolved to a smile. I believed the shooting star was a sign from heaven, a gift of hope from Bethany and from God. It was a reminder to me that Bethany was at home and at rest in heaven, and I found great comfort in that assurance. It was a respite from the cruel pain and loss I had felt for the past four days. The shooting star would become a sign of hope and comfort for me in the days to come, and I claimed it as my symbol of remembering my beautiful daughter.

The Gift of Time/ Hard Days at Home

Tony

Pain can be a blessing, even physical incapacity. My first weeks at home were adventures in discomfort. That was no pleasure, of course, but it did provide a distraction at times, allowing me to think of something other than the hole in my heart that was left when Bethany died.

The ribs still hurt whenever I moved, but my right arm was most aggravating. An orthopedist intern had put a soft cast of sorts on it when I came into the trauma room. Before I left the hospital, he took it off and left the arm in a sling, confident that the weight of my arm would be sufficient to keep the bones in line until they could begin healing. That never worked, however. The humerus was fractured at a sharp angle. I could manually pull the arm into place, but the muscles of my upper arm and shoulder inevitably pulled it apart, sliding the fractured ends over each other. The pain lessened, but it felt awkward to see and feel my arm bending as if it had two elbows, and it became obvious that it would not heal without help.

Eventually, we consulted another orthopedist who recognized the need for more aggressive treatment. On February 18, exactly one month after the wreck, I spent several days in a different hospital, where the orthopedist inserted a stainless steel rod (he called it an "intermedullary nail") into my upper arm, making an incision in my shoulder and driving the pin through the entire humerus and into the elbow.

One good friend offered a particularly healing ministry during those early weeks, both physically and emotionally. With my arm hanging down and relatively immobile, my right hand was constantly swollen from fluid that followed the course of gravity. The doctor prescribed a compression glove and suggested that someone could massage the hand, literally squeezing the fluid out of my hand and back into the arm, where it could be more readily absorbed.

When our friend Jill Keel came to visit, she would sit beside me and massage my bloated hand as we talked. Jill mainly listened. She knew it was therapeutic for me to voice what I was feeling emotionally—not just whether my ribs were still hurting. So, as her fingers gently pressed fluid from my hand, her questions prodded just deep enough to allow me to express inner feelings that many visitors didn't really want to hear.

From being on the receiving end, I learned anew that people who have experienced trauma or loss need a trusted minister or friend who is willing to take the time and invest the emotional energy to hear the deep stories of pain and fear that plague the soul. I didn't need that kind of ministry from everyone, but it was a special blessing to have a few friends who were willing to go the extra emotional mile. Jill did that for me, as did David Daly, a close friend from a minister support group to which both of us belonged. David lived on the other side of the state, so most of his listening was by phone, but no less meaningful.

Grace comes in many shapes and forms. Writing has been therapeutic for me since I was a teenager, but my back and arm prevented me from sitting at our desktop computer. Laptop computers were still a relative novelty in 1994, but a church friend who worked at IBM arranged the loan of an early model Thinkpad for me. I needed help getting set up, but could sit in the easy chair with that little computer in my lap and type to my heart's content. It was a godsend.

When reminders of Bethany seemed overwhelming, I tried to put them into words, often as poetry. One of the first things I noticed was that I became rather obsessed with thoughts of heaven. If I had not already believed in heaven, I would have invented it. I could not imagine that Bethany's light had gone out of the universe entirely. She was no longer with us, but I had to believe that something about her lived on. As a lifelong Christian, my thoughts naturally turned to the biblical concept of heaven.

The Bible says remarkably little about heaven, however. Revelation's description of jeweled gates, golden streets, and a sea of glass bear all the marks of metaphor. Jesus spoke of heaven as a place where God has prepared many dwelling places, but he did not describe them. The King James translation of "mansion" was of little help. I knew that the word could also mean "rooms."

I found myself imagining that heaven is very much like earth, except for the lack of tears and pain and death. I fantasized about what Bethany might be doing there. She had always wanted to ride a horse. Jan and I had talked about taking her riding when the weather warmed, but she died in winter, before we had the chance. The first poem I wrote, just twelve days after her death, began with the lines

I hope they have horses in heaven, and saddles and bridles and trails.
I hope they have puppies and kittens, and baseballs and hammers and nails.

I went on to list other things like pizza and fish sticks and French fries, things Bethany loved, things I hoped she would find in heaven. I suppose I was hoping she would feel at home there.

Anyone who has experienced the loss of a loved one knows how difficult holidays and other special days can be, especially through the first year, when the pain is still fresh and new.

Valentine's Day came less than a month after Bethany died. It's not really a major holiday, but is replete with reminders of sweethearts and love. I had always bought Bethany a box of candy and something special for Valentine's Day, but in 1994 that day of sweetness turned bitter. I spent part of the day shaping my emptiness into words, imagining that Bethany might be thinking of me, too. I wrote a long, meandering poem to express my love for her, hoping in some way that she might be aware of my thoughts.

As I pondered over the last few lines, a Cupid-red cardinal flew to the kitchen window and, seeing his reflection, began to peck at it. I fantasized that Bethany was communicating through the bird, sending a Valentine's Day message to assure me that she was in a better place and that she loved me, too.

That was not the last time I would imagine that Bethany was somehow trying to communicate with us. I have never been much of a mystic and have no confidence at all in those who claim they can communicate with the dead. Even so, I found my imagination working overtime in search of a sign that Bethany was happy and somehow whole.

At the same time, I realized that our lives would have to go on without her. We were in a desert time, but I had to believe that the rain would come again, that we would endure.

An invitation to visit two friends at their home in New Mexico gave Jan and me a chance to get away from the emptiness of our home and find a welcome change of pace. Nancy Curtis and Sara Ann Hobbs were early members at Woodhaven, staunch Baptists, and mission promoters of the best kind. We had walked far with them when Sara Ann suffered a severe stroke some years before. Now they reached out to walk with us by sending us plane tickets for a visit.

In early March, with my arm still in a sling, we flew to El Paso, Texas, where Nancy and Sara Ann picked us up for the long drive to their home in Silver City. The New Mexico desert was new to us. For several days, we ate Mexican food, visited ancient cliff dwellings, and rode through desert mountains hoping to catch a glance of bighorn sheep. We even drove south and crossed the border into Juarez just so we could say we had been to Mexico.

Contemplating the desert in the light of our life situation led me to reflect that the desert was a start-from-scratch, scratch-for-water kind of place, but there was life there, nonetheless. It offered a constant reminder of the hard lesson that the world is hard, but life goes on.

I wondered if that was why Elijah and Elisha, Jeremiah and John, even Jesus spent time in the wilderness. They needed to know that the world can be hard, but God remains present, and life goes on.

Looking over the arid land, pondering these things, I thought

Things that are true are taught time and again.
Now, here I stand on sun-baked sand—
the lesson is hard, but life goes on.

We returned home to confront another stressful day. March 9 is Bethany's birthday, and we knew that facing the first one would be hard. Friends came over to spend part of the day with us and share in remembering Bethany. Later, Jan and I drove to a cold, rainy cemetery where she released a bouquet of eight balloons while I took pictures of them drifting away.

Naturally, I tried to put some of what I was feeling into a poem bemoaning the loss of never celebrating another birthday with Bethany, and wondering whether such things were even remembered in heaven.

My attempts at poetry reflected typical struggles of dealing with grief. For all we learn about the "stages of grief" made famous by Elisabeth Kübler-Ross, the truth is that they are cyclical. One does not simply move in linear fashion from denial to questioning to acceptance. We may make progress from one to the other, but we may also circle back and start again, though generally for shorter periods.

On Valentine's Day, I was obsessed with thoughts of Bethany in heaven. In early March I was ready to accept the fact that life is hard, but it was time to move on. A week later, I was back in a sort of denial about Bethany's loss, knowing she was gone from earth but clinging to the tenuous connections of imagining her in heaven.

That would not be the last time. Sometimes we speak of making progress in terms of "three steps forward, two steps back." One can become discouraged when progress seems slow, but grief cannot be rushed. Recovery may seem slow in coming, but every dawdling step forward is a blessing in the making.

I could never quite shake my sense of obligation as pastor, even while Jan and I were officially on leave. Our church responded to Bethany's death magnificently, in many different ways. One of those ways was to offer both of us as much time off as we needed, trusting that we would not abuse the privilege, that we would come back to work as soon as we were able.

I wanted to share some of what I was learning even before returning to work, so I wrote an article for the church newsletter dated March 1, about six weeks after Bethany's death.

In the article, I described what it felt like to be a semi-invalid with a hole in the heart:

> I can't tie my shoes. I can't put on my belt or cut up my own meat. I can't hug my wife or your children with both arms. I can't lie on my side or my stomach, and I can't put my arms behind my head. As a result, even when I can't sleep, I can't toss and turn—I just shuffle my feet.
>
> I can't take a bath and get dressed without stopping to rest, and I can't walk more than a hundred yards before losing my breath. I can't do a thing to help Jan around the house, and sometimes I can't even get out of the easy chair without help. I can't get comfortable with being dependent and watching others take on my responsibilities.
>
> Most of all, I can't get used to the empty spot on the floor in front of our TV, or to the awful silence that comes from Bethany's room, or to eating breakfast alone.

The experience of loss, however, had led to an appreciation of blessings. So I wrote,

> I *can* be thankful that there is someone who is willing to tie my shoes, and to help with my belt, and to cut up my dinner. When I can't hug with two arms, I can be hugged with all the arms you have.
>
> While I lie in a rut and stare at the ceiling, I know that many of you are tossing and turning and praying in our behalf, just because you care.
>
> I can be thankful that you have been so willing to take up my slack, to help out around our house, and to rescue me from my chair. Sometimes you even bring your children over to make a little noise and give us a hug. I like that.
>
> In the midst of it all, I can know that we are loved by God and are in His care. I know that, because you prove it.

I never believed that God caused Bethany's death so that, by bringing tragedy into our lives, God could teach us something. At the same time, I could not imagine that God would ignore the opportunity to open new worlds to us in the midst of our grief, if only we were willing to listen, if only we were willing to learn.

※

Jan

The members of Woodhaven Baptist Church became our ministers following Bethany's death, sharing their presence with us through the most horrible event of our lives. They loved us and cared for us in significant and meaningful ways. The church family graciously granted us a leave of absence, not knowing how long it would be before we would return to minister among them. They told us to take all the time we needed, as they knew our bodies and hearts would not mend quickly.

The next few months would find me trying to hold it all together. I felt completely overwhelmed with all the tasks I faced each day. Tony was at home recovering from his physical injuries, and he spent most days sitting in a blue recliner with a laptop computer. Writing seemed to be the best means for expression of his grief. With his right arm broken, it was about the only thing he was able to do without great physical pain. He was also continuing to heal following surgery to insert a steel rod in his right arm.

I was dealing with the insurance companies, trying to secure the proper settlements to which we were entitled. Our insurance representatives, as well as those for the man who caused Bethany's death, were adding to an already stressful situation. There were requests for additional information that further delayed the settlement of insurance payments.

It seemed that each day I was on the phone either with our lawyer or a representative from Mothers Against Drunk Driving (MADD), keeping up with the latest news regarding the status of the upcoming hearing and trial for the man who had caused Bethany's death. I wanted us to be well-prepared for the court process and became somewhat obsessed with learning all that I could in preparation for dealing with a drunken driving case.

I was paying the bills, something that Tony had always done in the past. I had forgotten to make the car payment for the month of February and received a phone call a week after the due date. The caller informed me that a late fee would be added, but after I explained the events of the past month, he waived the fee. I found in those days that it was hard to concentrate on anything other than Bethany's death.

I was staying up very late at night, determined to write a personal thank-you note to every individual who had sent food or flowers or who had assisted us in special ways in the days following Bethany's death. I would build a fire each night and sit in a chair by the fireplace with my pen and note cards. As important as I thought this was, it took an enormous amount of time and emotional energy.

I was serving as the administrator of Bethany's estate and had to complete quite a bit of paperwork in this process. An estate checking account had to be opened at our bank, and any funds that we received related to Bethany's death, such as insurance settlements, had to be placed in this account. I was making regular trips to the courthouse in downtown Raleigh and dealing with matters with which I was unfamiliar. The county clerk was extremely helpful in assisting me. I had no idea that the death of my seven-year-old child would necessitate the settlement of her estate. The process seemed unnecessary and brought additional stress to my days.

I was also answering the phone and fielding inquiries about Tony's condition. It seemed that some who called asked questions related only to

Tony's recuperation and healing. I sometimes tired of telling the same story repeatedly and became somewhat resentful that some of the callers did not inquire as to how I was doing. I was thinking, "What about me? Don't you want to know how I'm doing?"

I shared with a friend how I was feeling about the phone calls. I was reminded that it was easier for some of the callers to inquire about Tony because they would just be given information. The caller would not have to deal with the emotions and the raw grief. This insight helped me know that people did care but oftentimes they just didn't know what to say or do for us.

A short time of respite did come for me at the end of February. The annual Youth Minister's Continuing Education retreat was held at Myrtle Beach. I had already made plans to attend but didn't think I should leave Tony alone. He had been home only a week after having the arm surgery, and I did not feel good about being away for four days. Tony, however, insisted that I go, knowing I needed a break from all that I had been dealing with during the last month. He was right, and I decided to attend.

The retreat provided me a time of rest and reflection. I roomed with Becky Knott, then youth minister at First Baptist Church in Smithfield. It was our good tradition to always request each other as roommates for this retreat. I will always be grateful for the time we had together those few days. Becky spent a lot of time listening to me as I shared my feelings about the events of the past month. She did not try to explain away my pain or tell me how I should be feeling. We spent the days in seminars and meetings, and we also took some time out for shopping and walking on the beach. Once back in our room in the evenings, Becky would ask me to share some of my favorite memories of Bethany. Becky seemed to know just what I needed as we spent those days together. These four days were a welcome respite for a tired wife and grieving mother.

Although we were officially on an indefinite leave of absence from Woodhaven, I did not entirely unplug from the church work and ministry responsibilities. I was still checking in at the office to see how things were going, and I was fielding calls from church members inquiring about Tony's recovery. I was also called upon to deal with a difficult situation within the youth group.

Hal Melton was leading the youth program during my absence. Three boys in the group were involved in a drug incident, and Hal called me to ask if I wanted to be present for a meeting with the youth and their parents. As their youth minister, I felt it was important for me to be involved even though I really did not have the emotional energy to deal with the situation. I resented having to deal with their adolescent problems in the midst of the overwhelming grief I was feeling at that time. I was also in the middle of preparing for the trial of the man who had killed Bethany. Even so, I agreed to meet with them. Hal, the youth, and their parents came to my home to discuss the matter.

I'm sure that had I not been grieving the death of my daughter, the tone of this meeting would have been quite different. I listened as the youth and their parents shared the details of the event. I was disappointed that the boys had made unwise decisions. Two of the boys were very remorseful for their actions. The other boy was arrogant and disrespectful to the adults in the room. My response to him was filled with anger. I know that much of the anger I expressed to him was misdirected. Even though I was disappointed and angry with him, the anger was really meant for the man who had killed Bethany. I had bottled up that anger for two months, but it came uncorked that day.

The months of February and March were filled with much activity and little time for personal reflection and grieving. I was spending a lot of time focusing on all the things Bethany would never experience. I thought about all the hopes and dreams that were taken from me as well. Bethany would never attend another year of school. I would miss giving her presents on her birthday and playing Santa Claus at Christmas. We would never go shopping at the Disney store in the mall and sing together while riding in the car. I would no longer get to help with homework or play games with her. I would no longer buy her favorite snacks at the grocery store.

I missed hugging her and tucking her in bed each night. Bethany would never enjoy another family vacation with us. She would never again ask me to kiss her "boo-boos" when she got hurt. I would never get to see her leave on her first date or attend a high school prom. Bethany would never be a high school senior wearing a graduation gown. I would miss filling out college applications with her. Bethany would never wear a wedding gown and marry. She would never have children, and I would never be a grandmother. My hopes and dreams for Bethany were buried with her in the grave.

I felt a tremendous amount of anger toward the person whose horrible choices had led to Bethany's death. He had entered our lives uninvited and unexpected, taking Bethany's life and transforming what was left of ours. I wished that he had been the one who died. He deserved it.

I was angry with God, and my prayers were mostly in the form of questions. Where were you? Why didn't you stop that truck from hitting our car? Why didn't you protect Bethany from harm? Why did you allow this to happen? What did I do to deserve this? I spent many restless nights raising my fist to the heavens and questioning the God who loved Bethany and me. I knew that God was present with me, but I was also feeling that God had somehow let me down. God had disappointed me by not sparing Bethany's life.

I was angry that Tony was still recovering from his injuries. I knew he didn't deserve the anger I felt toward him, but it was present. He was unable to assist with household chores. He couldn't drive when he wanted to get out of the house or had a doctor's appointment. Because of his injuries, he couldn't put his arms around me and hold me when I needed comforting. He couldn't wash the dishes, cook a meal, run the vacuum, or make up a bed. I was wearing too many hats. I was wife, maid, servant, chauffeur, cook, and nurse. I was doing it all and felt as though I was carrying a heavy burden alone. I was physically and emotionally exhausted. I was feeling very stressed and empty. I was angry that Bethany had been killed and that she was no longer with us. There was an empty chair at our table, and the void was huge.

I finally reached a boiling point on a Wednesday evening in early March. As we sat at the table eating dinner, I finally told Tony all that I was feeling. As the anger boiled over, I took my plate full of food and turned it over on the table. Tony just stared at me. I held my head down and salty tears fell into the London broil, rice, carrots, and green peas that now covered the table and the floor. Tony reached for my hand and held it as I cried. The floodgates had opened. I began sharing with him all the frustration, anger, and stress that had been bottled up inside me for the past six weeks.

And then the doorbell rang. Tony answered the door and invited in a friend from church who had stopped by to bring me a care package. I'm sure that she was surprised to see my dinner scattered all over my lap, the table, and the floor when she walked into the breakfast room. I was rather embarrassed as she sat down beside me. She listened patiently as we explained to her what had just happened. It was obvious that I was having a terrible, horrible, no good, very bad day.

I'm sure much of the stress and anger I was feeling at this time was also related to Bethany's approaching eighth birthday on March 9. This birthday was a reminder to me that Bethany would always be seven years old.

She would never celebrate another birthday here on earth. I would not get to see her grow up. Each birthday to come would be a stark reminder of the passing of another year and the void her absence left in my heart.

The first Mother's Day without Bethany would also be difficult, and I dreaded its coming. I did not feel like a mother anymore, though I knew that I would always be Bethany's mommy. The role of parent had been suddenly taken away from me. With no child to parent, I spent part of the day imagining what Bethany and I would have done together if she were here.

Mother's Day (May 8, 1994)

It is Mother's Day.
You are not here.
I wonder what you would say to me if you were.
I wonder what we would be doing together today.
You would wake me up by gently patting my arm.
Your big, sparkling blue eyes would dance with excitement
As you crawl in bed and snuggle next to me.
You would whisper, "Happy Mother's Day, Mommy."
You wouldn't stay still for long.
You would jump up and run to get the card and presents.
You would help me take off the ribbons and rip off the wrapping paper.
Your card would be filled with sentiments of your love
And signed in your second-grade handwriting.
We would go to church together.
You would make me a special gift
with your own hands during Sunday School
and hurry to place it in my hands before worship begins.
You would be so proud of your creation
And so would I
Because it came from your heart to mine.
Following church, we would go out to eat.
You would eat French fries and popcorn shrimp.
You would sit by me and occasionally
Rest your head in my lap.
At the end of the day
I would tuck you in bed.
We would read a bedtime story.
I would sing you a song.

We would kiss and say goodnight.
I would rub your tummy for a few minutes.
As I leave the room, I would hear you say as you often do,
"Mommy, you're the best mommy in the whole wide world.
I'm glad you are mine."
And I would say,
"Thank you, Bethany.
I'm glad you are mine. I love you. Goodnight, sleep tight."

chapter five

Return to the Land of the Living

Tony

Jan and I were blessed with many good friends and church members who truly knew how to minister to us. They reached out with love and grace, not trying to solve our problems or answer our questions, but simply offering the gift of presence. They sat with us, cried with us, and were not afraid to share their own memories of Bethany.

During this time we also received cards, letters, phone calls, and visits from hundreds of other well-wishers. Some of them brought truly comforting words and ministered to us with love and grace. Others who were just as well-meaning brought condolences we would rather not have heard.

There is something about a human that wants to explain things. We want to believe there is purpose in our living. Consequently, many people assume there must be a reason for everything that happens and often couch that belief in terms of God's will. An overzealous belief in providence leads many to the conviction that God directly causes all things, both good and bad, for God's own purposes.

Thus, we received multiple cards expressing the sentiment that God needed another angel in the heavenly choir or that we should rejoice because God only picks the loveliest flowers for His garden. Those sentiments, including the unfortunate allusion to our precious child as a decorative plant, were not helpful.

We came to realize that many people seemed more concerned with making themselves feel better than with comforting us. Some came bounding in with advice, encouraging us to think that the Lord had simply given us Bethany on loan for a while before "calling her home" because He needed her more than we did. We were assured that one day we would understand why this unspeakable event occurred because "God has a purpose for everything."

None of these well-wishers realized that such sentiments made us want to scream. Who wants to serve a God who treats parents like a greenhouse, simply parking a child with them until God needs the little one to fill a gap in God's flowerbed? Is that the way God works?

Visitors such as these reminded us of the friends who visited Job, ostensibly to comfort him after he lost all his children and most of his property and was afflicted with an ugly disease. His companions insisted that Job must have done something terrible to deserve what God had obviously done to him, while Job continued to maintain his innocence. Job's actions questioned the popular theology that God handed out blessings or curses in direct proportion to human obedience to the law.

It appears to me that the oft-stated conviction that everything happens for a God-ordained purpose grows out of an inadequate theology based more on imagination and folk-religion than on Scripture. Believing that God is all-knowing and all-powerful does not make Him all-responsible. God is responsible for creating the world and the people who dwell in it. Those people are responsible for the decisions they make.

The Bible teaches us that God created humankind "in his own image" (Gen 1:27), and one aspect of that image is the freedom of choice. We learn from the book of Genesis that God's children have made bad choices from the beginning.

We know that one person's bad choices can cause other people to suffer. It is not fair that the innocent should suffer for the sins of others, but *this is the price we pay for humanity.* If we had no human freedom to choose good or evil, we would all be like robots, unable to choose, unable to love, unable to laugh—or cry. We would then live as perpetual victims of an unfeeling fate, but God never intended that we be automatons. God created us with both freedom and responsibility—characteristics that cannot coexist with slavery to a divine puppet-master.

We often quote Romans 8:28: "And we know that God causes all things to work together for good to those who love God, to those who are called according to his purpose" (NASB). Many people assume this means that God is behind everything that happens, planning every event (even the horrible ones) for some good end. Assuming that God must have some good purpose for tragedy brings them comfort.

The truth of the text is not that all things are good, because they are not. Nor does it teach that all things happen according to God's purpose, because they do not. The great truth of this verse is that God is with us even in the vagaries, the uncertainties, and the tragedies of this world. And, because God is with us, God's amazing grace and unending love can bring goodness even from the worst of those things that happen.

Jan and I believe that God wept with us, that God shared our pain when our Bethany was killed—not by God's choice, but by a sinful man's bad choices. And we are confident that God has been working since that time to bring healing and hope to our lives. The spirit of Christ intercedes for us "with groanings too deep for words" (Rom 8:26), because there are no words for what we felt. Language alone cannot describe the loss of a child in her sunlit years of wonder.

We also believe that God's work in our behalf is most often done through the hearts and hands of God's people, and many have been agents of God's grace and love to us. The sharp and sometimes bitter taste of our experience led Jan and me to a desire to help others learn to be better agents of God's grace, rather than unwitting purveyors of added misery. So we collaborated on an article that was published in *Tar Heel Talk*, a newsletter for the North Carolina Woman's Missionary Union (WMU), and in *Contempo*, a magazine published by the national WMU organization.

We tried to explain, from the hurting person's perspective, how someone can best become the medium of God's gracious care.

The first gift, we said, was one of *presence*. Our most helpful friends were those who simply wanted to be there for us—not just before the funeral, but also for weeks afterward. They went to the store for us, took walks with us, listened to us, and cried with us. They never presumed to know the depth of our sorrow, but neither did they assume that this should keep them away. They were caring enough to be present when we needed them there and sensitive enough to be absent when we needed time alone.

We also urged potential comforters to show God's love with their *patience*. Our kindest friends did not grow weary with our grieving, nor did they expect us to jump back into our accustomed routines. They understood that something fundamental had changed and that we would never be the same people again. Those who loved us best were patient in allowing us to return to the land of the living at our own pace and in our own way.

Finally, we said, those who wish to bring comfort to the bereaved can mediate godly grace by being clear about their *purpose*. "Are you trying to comfort the bereaved," we asked, "or to comfort yourself? Do you come to share God's love or to defend God's reputation?"

Those who brought us the most comfort said things like "I love you," "I'm just here to walk with you," "I'm praying for you every day." There is no shame in saying, "I have no idea what to do or what to say, but I am here for you." Those who are bereaved rarely hear God speak in eloquent prose or rational arguments, but God's words sound clearly in the quiet tears of a friend who cares, in the still, small voice of unconditional love.

This is what Paul meant when he said "Bear one another's burdens, and so fulfill the law of Christ" (Gal 6:2). The law of Christ is the law of love. It is selfless love that stands in the place of another and does not fear their pain.

We concluded the article with these words: "What do you say when there's nothing to say? *You don't have to say anything at all.* Bring us your children to hug, sit by our side, hold on to our hand. The voice of healing speaks in many ways."

On March 13, a bit less than eight weeks after Bethany died, I returned to the pulpit at Woodhaven. The church allowed me to ease in rather slowly as my strength returned, but I was anxious to get back to work. We never felt unconnected from that wonderful community, but I had begun longing to feel more productive, to give something back. As much as I had needed ministry, I was tired of being ministered to and wanted to go back to being the minister.

The first sermon I preached on my return was an attempt to share some of the things I had learned through the tragic experience of losing a child. I called it "Lessons of the Heart." It was built around three of the many things I felt I had learned—or learned better—during the previous weeks.

I explained that the things I had learned were not so much "head knowledge" as *experiential* knowledge. I had learned what it feels like to lose a child without ever having a chance to say good-bye, the deep sense of a great inner void that constantly sucks at your soul and threatens to swallow you whole.

I had learned by experience what it felt like to have family and friends surround me with love and give me strength to fend off that internal vacuum and hope for better days.

I had also learned by experience a great many things about hospitals that I had previously known only by reputation. I knew about IVs and catheters and call buttons. I knew about chest tubes and bedpans and hospital food. I knew about epidural blocks that work full-time, and morphine pumps with a button that you can only push every five minutes. I knew about long lonely nights and hot tears in the morning.

While some lessons came from new experiences, others had come by *transference* from my head to my heart. By that I mean that there were things I had known for a long time, but they just didn't seem to matter much. I knew these truths in my head, but they had little effect on my heart.

That was true, at least, until Bethany died. Then they all came rushing forward.

In the sermon, I shared three things from that latter category—old truths that had left the realm of the abstract and settled themselves as concrete realities in the depths of my heart and soul.

The first of these was a lesson in the *absolute ugliness of sin.* From the time I was old enough to know what the word meant, I was taught that sin is an ugly thing. One of my mother's favorite commands was "Don't be ugly," and she wasn't talking about my looks.

I had seen through the years that sinful living leads to all kinds of unhappiness and ugliness. It had brought misery to my life before, and I had seen it bring sorrow to others. I had observed the struggles of families when one person's sin led to the suffering of others—of situations where children were abused or neglected because one or the other parent was irresponsible, or could not control their temper, or wasted their life on drinking or drugs.

I had been aware of stories such as these. I had preached about the dangers of sin and the need to be responsible. But I had been largely insulated from the ugliness of sin. I grew up in a functional, healthy family. I was blessed with a loving wife and good children. I didn't go to dangerous places or hang out with violent people. Without consciously thinking about it, I assumed that my family was safe.

And then one cold morning while Bethany and I were safely and nicely minding our own business, I learned from experience that someone else's sin and ugliness can reach out and involve you whether you like it or not. You don't have to go looking for trouble. Trouble will often come looking for you.

There is a verse in the book of Romans that I have quoted many times. It begins with these words: "The wages of sin is death" (Rom 6:23). While I have always known that sin could lead to physical death, I had always interpreted that verse as a reference to eternal death alone. Those who choose to live in sin will face an eternal death.

And that is an appropriate interpretation. But after Bethany's death I began to see that verse in a new light. I will never hear the words "the wages of sin is death" in the same way again. Our innocent child paid the wages for another man's sin. The price she paid was death, and all who loved her paid with grief and loss.

This says something to me about personal responsibility. I am not just responsible for myself when I am tempted to sin; I am responsible for others, too. The man who killed our daughter did not intend to hurt anyone and surely never thought he would kill a child. He thought he could drink one or two beers and not be affected by them. He thought he could drink three or four or five and still drive his truck, but he was wrong—and we are the ones who paid.

That is the way temptation works. That little voice inside says, "It's okay to make yourself happy. You're not hurting anybody else. You can drink that beer—one beer never hurt anybody. You can cheat on your wife—what she doesn't know won't hurt her. You can steal from the company—they'll never miss it. You can ignore your neighbor's needs—what did they ever do for you? You can keep all your income for yourself—the church would probably just waste it. You can buy anything you want or do anything that feels good because after all, what you want is all that really matters."

That little voice doesn't have to speak loudly, because it is saying what we want to hear, and it is so easy for us to agree. But somewhere, somehow, we have got to hear another voice. A true voice. The one that says, "The wages of sin is death!"

The second lesson I mentioned, a truth that had gone from head to heart, was *the centrality of the Christian hope.* We find that hope in the other half of Romans 6:23. The wages of sin may be death, "but the gift of God is eternal life, through Jesus Christ, our Lord."

I first began to comprehend the need for salvation and the hope of heaven when I was eight or nine years old. One reason I chose to follow Christ is that I wanted to be saved from eternal death and to experience eternal life in heaven. Once I made that choice and followed Christ in baptism, I felt assured that my sins were forgiven, my soul was safe, and there was a home in heaven for me. The matter seemed settled, and I didn't give it a lot more thought.

In years since, my service as a minister often led me to proclaim the good news of salvation. In officiating at scores of funeral services, I sought to reassure bereaved family members that their loved ones were at home with Christ in a better, eternal world.

I don't want to suggest that I did this without compassion or genuine concern for those families, but my understanding of their grief was limited because I had never lost anyone as close to me as a parent, or a child, or a spouse.

Thoughts of heaven rarely factored into my daily living because I wasn't there yet and didn't anticipate being there soon. All the people who mattered most to me were still on earth.

But in those first weeks after Bethany's death, I said to the church family, "I think about heaven all the time now. It matters to me now. I can't tell you how much it matters. That little blond-headed girl who used to put her arm around my leg and walk up the aisle with me after church isn't *here* anymore. She is *there*, in heaven, probably putting her arms around Jesus' leg and following Him around."

Or so I hoped. I realized that, if I had not already believed in the concept of heaven, I would have invented it. I could not bear the thought that Bethany no longer existed in some way, that her spirit was not still alive and in a better place. And so I held on to hope in Christ's love for innocent children and the promise to receive his own and bring them into his Father's house. There were days when I felt that such hope was all that stood between me and insanity.

So I began to cling to every promise of heaven, to every reassurance that we who love Christ will one day be together again. And we do have such promises in Scripture. We don't have to make up our own version of heaven as a temporary psychological crutch; God has inspired others to record God's promises to us.

We have the promise Jesus made to his disciples at the Last Supper, as John records it: "In my Father's house there are many dwelling places. If it were not so, would I have told you that I go to prepare a place for you? And if I go and prepare a place for you, I will come again and will take you to myself, so that where I am, there you may be also" (John 14:2-3).

We have the promise Jesus made to the thief on the cross: "Truly I tell you, today you will be with me in Paradise" (Luke 23:43).

We have Paul's assurance that there is a better life beyond this one: "For we know that if the earthly tent we live in is destroyed, we have a building from God, a house not made with hands, eternal in the heavens" (2 Cor 5:1).

We have the writer of Revelation's majestic description of how it will feel to be in heaven: "And I heard a loud voice from the throne saying, 'See, the home of God is among mortals. He will dwell with them as their God; they will be his peoples, and God himself will be with them; he will wipe every tear from their eyes. Death will be no more; mourning and crying and pain will be no more, for the first things have passed away'" (Rev 21: 3-4).

I had to believe such promises were true, that heaven is real, that Bethany is there. At age seven, she had not made a public profession of faith, but she had talked openly about her belief in God. Though she had asked about being baptized, we had encouraged her to wait until she had a greater understanding of what it meant to make a life-choice to follow Christ.

There were many things Bethany did not yet understand, but what her faith lacked in maturity, it made up for in purity. She could have been one of the children that Jesus held up as an example to his disciples: "People were bringing little children to him in order that he might touch them; and the disciples spoke sternly to them. But when Jesus saw this, he was indignant and said to them, 'Let the little children come to me; do not stop them; for it is to such as these that the kingdom of God belongs. Truly I tell you, whoever does not receive the kingdom of God as a little child will never enter it.' And he took them up in his arms, laid his hands on them, and blessed them" (Mark 10:13-16).

In the first weeks after Bethany's death, nothing mattered more to me than the belief that she was in a place where Jesus could take her into His arms and bless her. I pondered the details—wondering if she could still play sports, or eat cheese pizza, or paint rainbows—and though I could not know those things, the hope Christ offers was sufficient.

The third truth I shared was a deeper awareness of *the ultimate importance of human choice*. The choices we make about our behavior reach far beyond our own skin. Our choices can bring good or evil into the world, can bring joy or pain, life or death.

That is something I had known in my head, but Bethany's death shoved it into my heart. I learned the importance of stopping from time to time to examine the choices we make so easily—and often thoughtlessly. Do my choices bring joy and love and life to others, or could they lead to pain and hurt and death?

One of those choices has to do with our own life, and our death, and what there is beyond death. One option is destruction. When Paul spoke of those who rejected God, he said, "Their end is destruction; their god is the belly; and their glory is in their shame; their minds are set on earthly things" (Phil 3:19).

When Jesus talked about the choices we make, he gave this advice: "Enter through the narrow gate; for the gate is wide and the road is easy that leads to destruction, and there are many who take it. For the gate is narrow and the road is hard that leads to life, and there are few who find it" (Matt 7:13-14).

Destructive choices are seductively easy to make, but Jesus calls us to choose life. That is why Jesus took on human form, why he suffered, why he died for us: "For God so loved the world that he gave his only Son, so that everyone who believes in him may not perish but may have eternal life. . . . Very truly, I tell you, anyone who hears my word and believes him who sent me has eternal life, and does not come under judgment, but has passed from death to life" (John 3:16; 5:24).

All of which brings us back to Romans 6:23: "For the wages of sin is death, but the free gift of God is eternal life in Christ Jesus our Lord."

Moses once stood before a ragtag bunch of sinful people and explained to them the ways of good choices and bad choices. He concluded with this challenge: "I call heaven and earth to witness against you today that I have set before you life and death, blessings and curses. Choose life so that you and your descendants may live, loving the LORD your God, obeying him, and holding fast to him; for that means life to you and length of days . . ." (Deut 30:19-20a).

We can choose life or death. We can choose to live in community or alone. We can choose to be givers or takers. We can choose to bring joy or pain to others.

There are times when we feel invulnerable, and thoughts of what lies beyond are far from our consciousness. There are times when it is easy to think of ourselves and not of others. There may be times when we think such choices do not matter, but there are no such times. Our choices matter, and they matter now.

We are not promised tomorrow—another lesson of the heart. I had read James 4:14 before the day our daughter began one journey and finished another one, but it was on that day when I fully understood that "You do not even know what tomorrow will bring. What is your life? For you are a mist that appears for a little while and then vanishes."

It seems a bit ironic that we cannot count on tomorrow, but we *can* count on eternity—if we understand the terminal ugliness of sin and choose to follow the road to life, the road that is marked by the small but sturdy signs of our Christian hope.

✻

Jan

As Tony preached this sermon, I was reminded of Bethany's usual habit of wrapping her arms around Tony's leg and walking up the aisle with her daddy during the benediction song. She was not here today to do that with him. Following Tony's benediction prayer, I walked to the front of the church and reached for his hand. As the congregation sang, we walked up the aisle hand in hand, very aware of the absence of our blonde-headed little girl.

We slowly made our way back to the land of the living. There was still an emptiness and sadness that enveloped me over the next few months. I had no energy. I wanted to stay in bed each morning rather than get up and live in a world without Bethany. I was feeling depressed and becoming more aware that I needed help to sort through all that I had bottled up inside of me. In April, I made an appointment with a professional counselor I had seen in the past. I trusted her and knew she could help me work through this overwhelming grief. I would continue to see her on a weekly basis for the next year.

I was still spending a lot of time focusing on the upcoming hearing for Darrell, the man who caused Bethany's death. I talked regularly by phone with the prosecuting attorney in Chesterfield, South Carolina. Donna Carter, Victim Services Coordinator with MADD of Darlington, South Carolina, called frequently to keep us informed on the status of the case. She was instrumental in helping us prepare for the hearing and the trial. Her tireless efforts on our behalf were appreciated as we sought justice through the court system.

My brother Ben located a friend from our childhood who is now an attorney in Columbia, South Carolina. He agreed to work on our case with the prosecuting attorney in Chesterfield. We felt that we needed to hire our own legal representative, as we had heard many horror stories about the "good old boy" system of lawyers that operated in Chesterfield County. We wanted to make sure our case was handled properly and justly.

I also spent time and energy thinking about Darrell, the man responsible for Bethany's death. He had made a terrible choice to drink and drive. Bethany was dead as a result of his actions. I wished that he had been the one who had died in the wreck. I was furious that this stranger had crashed uninvited into our lives and inflicted pain upon us. He had taken our daughter away from us. I was angry that he was not in jail. I wanted him punished for the pain he had brought upon Bethany and our family.

In one of my counseling sessions, I talked about the anger I was feeling. My counselor invited me to take a large foam bat in my hands. She placed a pillow in a chair and asked me to pretend that it was Darrell. She then told me to tell and show him what I was feeling. I took the bat and began hitting the pillow as hard as I could, pounding repeatedly as I called Darrell unprintable names that I don't normally use. I told him I hated him, and I wished him dead. After a few minutes of beating the pillow and the chair, I fell to the floor in a fetal position. I stayed there and cried as my counselor held my hand. We were silent for a long while as the hot, salty tears stung my face. It was a welcome release to finally give expression to the deep anger that had been eating away at me for months.

Tony and I also did couple's counseling with my counselor and one of her colleagues. We were very aware of the statistics that indicate many marriages end in divorce following the death of a child, though we think the numbers may be exaggerated. Many of those marriages may have already been in trouble, and the death of the child served to add more stress to the relationship. We were proactive in seeking counseling. We wanted to take preventive measures to keep ourselves from becoming another couple whose marriage fell apart after a child died.

It was in our counseling sessions together that we were able to draw closer to one another as we shared our concerns, fears, and hopes. In one session, Tony was able to voice his continuing fear that I might blame him for Bethany's death. He was already dealing with his own doubt and fear that perhaps he had not done all he could to avoid the wreck, even with the knowledge that the wreck was caused by a drunken driver. I was able to assure him that I had never blamed him, and I would never find reason to believe that the wreck was his fault.

Spending time with a professional counselor also helped me to be able to share with Tony on a deeper level. I became more open and responsive, more willing to let myself be known. We were able to be vulnerable and honest and acknowledge the great loss we both had experienced. We found that as we shared our grief, our relationship was strengthened. This proved to be a time of enrichment and growth for both of us.

My past tendency when dealing with grief was to turn inward and shut down emotionally. I learned this behavior when I was eleven years old. In 1969, my forty-eight-year-old father died from a massive heart attack in the kitchen of our home in South Carolina. Six months later, my mother, brother, and I moved to Reidsville, North Carolina, where our extended family lived.

I had been dealt a tremendous blow at the age of eleven, and I had no idea how to deal with the loss. Few adults were willing to talk with me about what I was feeling. My mother's grief was overwhelming, my brother was enrolled in a military school away from home, and my grandparents were heartbroken. I don't think there was ever any discussion about the possibility of me seeing a counselor to get assistance in understanding my grief. I felt lonely and turned my grief inward.

From that time on I shut down emotionally. This pattern of shutting down would also invade other relationships in my life. At times when I felt hurt, pain, or rejection, I would shut down, unable to express what I was feeling. I was unable to be vulnerable with others and scared of getting too close to another person for fear that they would die and leave me as my father had. I wasn't able to share my honest feelings with those who wanted to know me on a deeper level. I had become lost to myself. It would take many years and some time in counseling during my adult life for me to finally let the walls down that I had built around my heart.

Following Bethany's death, I knew I wanted to work through and walk through my grief in a different way. I didn't want to run from it or hide my emotions. When Bethany died, a community of faith surrounded me, something that was lacking when my father died. The Woodhaven family provided a safe environment in which I could share the raw emotions, anger, and pain that I felt. I felt safe crying openly when the waves of grief would come over me, even if it happened during a Sunday morning worship service. This support system would allow me to share a grief that ran deep. I was given the permission and the space to grieve in healthy and growing ways.

In the aftermath of Bethany's death, I tried not to run from my feelings. Although I did a lot of internal processing of all that was going on within and around me, I was careful to let Tony and others know how I was doing, what I was feeling, and what I needed. Friends and family members were willing to sit and listen to me talk, even when they didn't know what to say or do. I was not embarrassed to admit that I needed to see a professional counselor. I could not walk this path of grief alone. The old pattern of withdrawing and shutting down would not be a means of survival for me this time. I had learned that if I wanted to move forward to healing and hope, I would need to give voice to the deep groanings of my heart. This not only allowed me to survive, but to thrive.

In the past I had written songs as a means of expressing feelings and thoughts. Several years before, I had written a song for a young man named Matthew who was in the youth group at Woodhaven. His father died from cancer a few years before Bethany's death. Though written for Matthew, the song took on new meaning for me when Bethany died. Perhaps it speaks even to what I was feeling when I was eleven years old, but unable to voice at that time.

Walk with Me (Matthew's Song)

How do you know what I feel inside?
How can you share this pain?
How can you see beyond the smile I wear?
It's easy to say that you understand,
Easy to walk away;
Harder to say, "You know I really care."

(chorus)
I need you to look within,
I need you to be my friend,
I need a hand to hold that's always there.
I need you to let me cry
And listen to the question, "Why?"
Walk with me through days that don't seem fair.

I hear you saying that it's all right,
Everything is okay,
But somehow your words don't touch the hurt inside.
So many questions inside my head,
Answers are hard to find;
I want someone to hear me when I say . . .

(repeat chorus)

All of us will face days when life does not seem fair, days when we need others to walk with us and hold our hand. When those days come, we need to allow others to minister to us, even as we seek to comfort them when they face their own trials.

chapter six

Into the Courtroom: Confronting a Killer

Tony

The months following Bethany's death were filled with a series of unpleasant duties that often peeled back the scabs of our grief, inflicting new pain. The personal issue of dealing with tragic loss is consuming enough, but the aftermath of loss can be far more complicated. There are estate matters to deal with, for example, and funeral home bills to pay, and insurance settlements to negotiate. In our case, there was also the matter of preparing for a court trial.

Since I was slowed by physical injuries for about two months after the wreck, Jan took the lead in dealing with the estate issues. I wouldn't have thought that a seven-year-old could have much of an estate to deal with, but the legal steps of recording her death and directing what would became of her possessions were still necessary. Bethany, like most seven-year-olds, did not have a will, so her "estate" of teddy bears, toys, clothing, and a small college account had to be officially probated. A death certificate and several copies had to be obtained for various purposes.

None of this was pleasant—every legal step was an additional reminder that Bethany was gone, and every trip to the courthouse was another drain on our emotions and energy. I was thankful that Jan was willing to handle these matters, and very proud of the way she stepped up and dealt with hard things in a mature and efficient manner. I was also grateful to the staff in the Wake County probate department, who were unfailingly courteous and compassionate in leading us through the legal aspects of death's aftermath.

I wish I could say the same for our insurance company, which became a source of grating irritation and renewed grief. We had no life insurance on Bethany, but our automobile insurance policy included a rider providing payments in the event of specific injuries or deaths resulting from a crash. One might assume that such payments would be automatic, but that was not the case.

The driver who caused Bethany's death had a similar policy, and his insurance company paid the stated amount without complaint. They were not quick about it and may have chosen not to argue in hopes that we would not sue for a larger amount, but I prefer to believe they simply acknowledged appropriate responsibility for the claim and paid it.

When we filed a claim with our own insurance company, however, the story was different. The company we used is nationally known, particularly popular in rural areas. It is not a fly-by-night operation. Yet, instead of standing behind their long-term customers, they seemed to make every effort to avoid paying.

The first hint of trouble came with the initial call from the company's adjuster. Before the company would pay, he said, we would have to provide a certified death certificate, a transcript of Bethany's schoolwork, and written statements about her character from her teachers. I was outraged and pressed for why the company should need anything beyond a death certificate, but he was persistent. When asked why the additional documentation was needed, he hemmed and hawed about wanting some indication of how Bethany might have turned out if she had lived. He seemed to be trying to place a value on our daughter's life, based on her future prospects.

I don't get mad easily, but I was deeply incensed by this. It was not as if we were dealing with a lawsuit asking compensatory damages based on a person's earning prospects if they had not been killed. The policy called for a certain amount to be paid if someone died in a crash, period. It was not hard for us to demonstrate that Bethany was a good student, with good character, beloved by teachers and classmates alike. But that should have been irrelevant as far as the insurance company was concerned. If she had failed every class and tormented her teachers, the company would have had no grounds for refusing to pay the small settlement called for in the policy.

I suspect the adjuster was following a standard company checklist and asking for far more information than was required, because the company probably does face occasional lawsuits in which people seek more damages than called for in the policy. Even so, we felt that the company was being inflexible and heartless in requiring us to jump through a number of painful and unnecessary hoops, as if hoping we would surrender the claim rather than pushing through their onerous requirements. I called our agent and wrote letters to company officials expressing our concerns. Eventually, we received the settlement, but there was never a single word of apology from the company. Not surprisingly, we took our business elsewhere.

The trial of Darrell is another matter altogether. As our insurance company sought to evade its obligations, the man who caused Bethany's death tried every means at his disposal to avoid taking responsibility for his actions. Naturally, this generated a great deal of frustration and anger on our part. The highway patrol had clearly faulted him for causing the wreck. His blood alcohol level was more than twice the legal limit, even hours after the wreck. We were amazed that he could consider anything other than pleading guilty and begging for the mercy of the court.

What hurt so badly, however, is that his attempt to dodge responsibility seemed to discount the gravity of what he had done, as if he did not think causing a child's death was something to be taken seriously.

We learned later that this was a familiar pattern. Darrell had been arrested for drunken driving, or for causing an accident while drunk, on multiple occasions. Yet, with the help of his father and his lawyer (a cousin), he had been able to repeatedly negotiate the "good old boy" network in the county court system and get almost all of the charges dropped by paying small fines. Apparently, he thought the lawyer could come through for him again.

We were determined that this would not happen. Here was a repeat offender who had killed a child, at least in part because the local justice system had not held him accountable for earlier infractions. He had been guilty of drunken driving many times before. He had even been arrested for it. But he had never lost his license, gone to prison, or received a significant enough penalty to make an impact. As a result, he kept drinking and kept driving until he killed someone.

We didn't want him to kill anyone else.

After we learned that he sought a trial rather than offering a guilty plea that could have brought some closure to the matter, we were faced with legal preparations. We were asked to fill out lengthy "victim impact statements," for example, explaining in detail how Bethany's death and my injuries had impacted our lives.

We were also given contact information for the Chesterfield County solicitor (similar to a district attorney in other states). After obtaining copies of Darrell's driving records and hearing (via unsolicited phone calls from his ex-wife) troubling stories about how he had managed to slip through the justice system unscathed, we decided to hire a lawyer to assist the county solicitor. It wasn't so much that we didn't trust the county solicitor, but we wanted to make sure no stone was left unturned. Even though this would cost us thousands of dollars that we would not attempt to recover through a civil suit, we felt that we owed it to Bethany, to ourselves, and to everyone else who travels the highways in that part of the world to do all we could to get Darrell off the road.

*

Jan

The man who killed Bethany was twenty-nine years old at the time of the crash. He lived in a mobile home outside of Hartsville, South Carolina, and worked a shift job in nearby Cheraw. On January 18, 1994—as Bethany and Tony were preparing to begin their drive home from Georgia—he left work at 7:00 AM and made his way to Billy's Beer and Wine, a bar located about two blocks from his workplace. The small tavern opened early each morning to cater to the third-shift employees.

Darrell spent at least four hours at the bar drinking Bud Ice, a beer with twice the alcohol content of regular beer. He then made the horrible choice to get in his aging black pickup truck and attempt to drive home. He later claimed that he drank only three beers over the four-hour period, but a hospital blood test two hours after the wreck showed his blood alcohol content to be .203, more than twice the legal limit.

In the months following Bethany's death, we not only had to deal with the grief and pain of her loss, but we also had to endure a journey through the court system. The first step was a preliminary hearing held on April 18, 1994. The wreck had occurred in Chesterfield County, South Carolina, so court was held at the courthouse in Chesterfield, the county seat.

We were not required to be present at the hearing, but we were not convinced that justice would be done without our active participation in the process. When we arrived that morning, Donna Carter, with MADD, met us in the parking lot. Her presence during the hearing provided support and encouragement, and her knowledge of the local court process in drunken driving cases was invaluable.

Once inside the courthouse, we passed through a security check, entered the courtroom, and seated ourselves on one of the long church-style pews. We had never seen Darrell, did not know what he looked like, and did not realize that he and his family were seated directly behind us.

When the judge called for his case and asked Darrell to enter a plea, he stood and hovered over us as he effectively pleaded "not guilty" to killing our daughter. He could not bring himself to actually say the words "not guilty," but simply mumbled, "I'd like a trial." It amounted to the same thing, however, as his request for a trial was entered as a "not guilty" plea for the court record.

I had carried an 8-x-10-inch photograph of Bethany with me. Once the hearing was over, I stood up, turned around, and confronted Darrell. I held Bethany's picture in front of him and said, "I just want you to see what you took from us." He hung his head and said nothing. I turned and saw a highway patrolman quickly making his way from the other side of the courtroom toward me. The patrolman took me by the arm and calmly explained that my confrontation might jeopardize the impending trial. He understood my pain, he said, but he wanted to make sure that justice would be served.

We learned, in time, that he and several other patrolmen had long been frustrated by Darrell's ability to slip through the court system. They had arrested him on multiple occasions, only to see him evade the charges or escape with minor fines. The patrolmen, like us, wanted Darrell convicted and off the road, so I was urged to not say or do anything else that might jeopardize the case.

We obtained a copy of Darrell's driving record, which included no less than six previous incidents that had resulted in either property damage or personal injuries. He could have received a total of sixteen points on his license if convicted for all of these incidents, but had accumulated only three points for a single conviction of reckless driving. A local magistrate had handled the cases, occasionally imposing fines but never suspending Darrell's license or restricting his driving.

When Darrell left the hospital two days after the wreck, his father posted the $10,000 bail for him to remain free. We were told that the magistrate instructed him to attend church every Sunday and abstain from alcohol, but he was still allowed to drive.

Darrell had been able to get off easy in the past. We wanted to make sure that the seventh incident resulted in a conviction, in prison time served, and in the loss of his driver's license.

During the next month we had several conversations and interviews with the prosecuting attorney and the lawyer we had hired. They purchased photographs of the accident, with Bethany still buckled into her seat, from the man Tony remembered taking pictures shortly after the wreck. One photo of Bethany was blown up poster-size, in case it was needed as a visual aid for the jury, illustrating the violence of the wreck and the extent of Bethany's injuries. Tony and I did not see the photographs, nor did we ask to view them. Just knowing they were in the room was hard enough.

The trial was finally scheduled to begin on June 29, 1994. Tony and I were scheduled to attend a youth conference at the beach with the Woodhaven youth group during that same week. We spent the first part of the week with the youth at the North Carolina Baptist Assembly, commonly known as "Caswell" because of its location on the grounds of the former Fort Caswell, near the southeast corner of the state. The group prayed with us and sent us on our way to Chesterfield on Wednesday morning of that week.

We were glad for the company of Tony's parents and a number of friends that day, many of them wearing buttons with a picture of Bethany's sweet face and the words "I remember Bethany." This time, there was less concern about bumping into Darrell or his family. Our supporters and we were seated on the right side of the courtroom, while Darrell and his girlfriend, parents, and grandparents sat behind his attorneys on the other side.

Much of the morning was spent in the courtroom, watching the tedious process of jury selection. Darrell's lawyer sought to strike jurors that he thought would not be sympathetic to his case, while our lawyer and the district attorney did the opposite. Like any defense lawyer, Darrell's attorney had hopes of drawing a jury that might favor acquittal, but when the last member of the jury was seated, he was apparently not optimistic about the prospects.

Darrell's attorney requested a brief recess and huddled with his client, then with our lawyer and the prosecuting attorney. Our lawyer consulted with us, explaining that they were working on a plea bargain agreement. We were told that Darrell was willing to plead guilty if they asked for a sentence of no more than twelve to fifteen years in prison. There were no guarantees, but the attorneys thought the judge would agree to at least twelve years. We thought this was reasonable and added our endorsement, relieved that there might be no need for a further trial.

After the recess, the judge accepted the plea, then invited family members and friends on both sides to express their feelings prior to sentencing.

Darrell's elderly but outspoken grandfather was the first to speak. He stood up and blamed all of his grandson's problems, including his drinking, on Darrell's ex-wife, refusing to place any responsibility for the crime on his grandson. The grandfather then looked directly at our family and told the judge that if we were the Christians that we professed to be, we would offer to forgive Darrell and not press for him to be punished. The man pleaded with the judge to be lenient on his grandson and spare him a prison sentence. His words angered me.

Darrell's mother had sent a sympathy card to us several months earlier, acknowledging that the entire family shared in his guilt. This was another example of the family refusing to hold Darrell accountable for his actions. But neither Darrell's mother nor father spoke during the trial. Both appeared to be too overcome with emotion to speak.

Darrell chose not to speak in his own behalf. His attorney explained that he was distraught and unable to speak to the court. The lawyer told the judge that Darrell was very sorry for his actions and asked him to consider his client's sincere remorse when handing down the sentence.

We were then given an opportunity to share our "victim impact statements," explaining how Darrell's actions had affected and changed our lives. Paper copies of the statements were filed with the court, but Tony and I also spoke to the judge and those present in the courtroom, telling how our lives had been changed as a result of Bethany's death and Tony's injuries.

After we spoke, Janice shared how the children at Woodhaven had been affected by the loss of their friend. Jill Keel explained how her daughter Molly had been hurt by the death of her best friend and playmate. Mama Hollie described the pain that she and Daddy Bill had endured in the loss of a grandchild. As each of us spoke, Darrell stood to our left a few feet away, with his head down. He would not even look at us. He never spoke a word before his sentencing.

The judge then pronounced the sentence, convicting Darrell on two felony counts of driving under the influence (DUI), one for Bethany's death and one for Tony's injuries. The judge imposed two twelve-year prison terms, to run concurrently. After sentencing, Darrell was handcuffed and led away by a sheriff's deputy. His mother, father, girlfriend, and grandparents were crying and immediately retreated to the hallway to say their good-byes to Darrell.

I remember looking up behind the judge and reading the biblical words of Amos inscribed on the courthouse wall: "Let justice roll down like waters, and righteousness like an ever-flowing stream" (Amos 5:24, NASB). I believed that justice had rolled down in the courtroom that day. Tears were streaming down my face, too, as Darrell was led away to prison.

Tony and I spent time with our friends after the sentencing, and then we returned to Caswell, grateful that we could put the matter behind us, at least until the first parole hearing. As we drove up to the cottage at Caswell, we noticed that a large hole had been dug in the front yard, with a small live oak tree standing near the hole, waiting to be planted. Bethany had always loved both Caswell and the youth group at Woodhaven, and the youth wanted to plant a tree in her memory. The Caswell staff knew Bethany, too. They not only gave permission but also kindly purchased the tree.

The following afternoon, we gathered with the youth and adult chaperones in a circle around the tree and remembered Bethany with stories that brought smiles to our faces. I read Ecclesiastes 3:1-8, which speaks of a time to live and a time to die, a time to weep and a time to rejoice. We each took a turn at shoveling dirt around the tree's roots, and the youth helped Caswell staffers stake it down and add an irrigation hose. We would later place a granite marker at the foot of the tree, inscribed "In memory of our special friend and mascot, Bethany Rush Cartledge."

It felt good to be surrounded by those who were also special friends to us as we closed this chapter in our journey toward healing.

Learning to Survive/ We Will Survive

Tony

1994 began under the black cloud of Bethany's death, and it remained cloudy for a long time. Working through legal and administrative issues like Bethany's estate, insurance settlements, and the drunk-driving trial were like so many obstacles that needed to be cleared, with one coming after the other. Each one took time, involving multiple hurdles and many careful steps in between. Jan opened an estate account within weeks of Bethany's death, but it wouldn't be closed out until October. Contact with the insurance companies began in February, but the last payment wasn't made until August. The man who caused Bethany's death in January was sent to prison in June, but by September we were writing letters opposing his bid to get out on work release.

As these things filled our plate, we also gradually reengaged in our work at Woodhaven and tried to return to some semblance of normal life. But life was not normal, nor close to it. At every turn, we tripped and fell into empty holes left by Bethany's departure.

What should we do with her clothes? With her toys? With her room? With her memories?

We tackled the clothes first, as I recall. Most of the everyday clothes we boxed up, though they remained in her closet, along with other boxed toys and treasures. But it was hard to hide those little Sunday dresses, so many of them given to her by her two grandmothers, all of them chock-full of memories. Phyllis Yelvington, a dear friend and an excellent quilter, offered to make a "memory quilt" with pieces cut from the dresses, and we readily agreed. Phyllis and several of her quilting friends produced three beautiful and creative quilted wall hangings. We kept one and gave the others to our parents.

Jan had adopted a shooting star as her symbolic way of remembering Bethany, and I adopted the teddy bear. I had bought many bears for Bethany, often purchased when traveling, and she liked them. I began to look for neckties that featured teddy bears. Two friends gave me teddy bear tiepins, and I often wore one of them on my lapel. After I began to drive again, one of her stuffed teddy bears sat on the seat beside me for months, and I often held it in my lap as I drove.

But what to do with the rest of Bethany's bears and toys, the many games, the few dolls, the art supplies, and the little jewelry boxes that held her hair clips and ribbons? We gave a few of Bethany's stuffed animals to other children who had been close to her so they could have a personal remembrance, but we simply could not bring ourselves to clean out her room.

That is every parent's nightmare, I suppose. In fact, Jan and I had discussed that very thing the previous November after a teenager who attended our youth group was killed when she ran a stop sign and was hit by another driver. We tried to envision what it would be like to face the prospect of having to clean out Bethany's room if something were to happen to her. We imagined that it would be devastating, and we imagined correctly.

As a result, we hardly touched Bethany's room for nearly a year. The blue painted walls, the bunny rabbit border near the ceiling, the piggy bank and jewelry box on her dresser remained as they were when she last saw them. The bunk beds she loved to climb on stood firm, neatly made, and covered with stuffed animals. We did not close the door—in fact, we insisted on keeping it open—but the Christmas season would be near before we could bring ourselves to pack up most of her toys and make any changes in the room.

Memories of Bethany stuck to us like fine beach sand on wet feet, and we welcomed them. Indeed, we felt as if we could not live without them, though we also knew that we must move beyond being obsessed and possessed by memories.

We, and others, chose a variety of public ways to remember Bethany, and all of them were comforting to us. This began with her grave marker. Bethany is buried in a memorial garden that requires all grave markers to be flat bronze plaques of a certain size. We had a marker custom made to feature a teddy bear (for me) holding a bunch of balloons (for Jan), and the inscription "of such is the kingdom of God."

In the previous chapter, we mentioned the tree that the Woodhaven youth group planted near Yucca Cottage where we usually stayed during summer camp at Caswell. Earlier, within weeks of Bethany's death, her second-grade class at West Lake Elementary School had also dedicated a blossoming cherry tree in her memory. In helping her classmates cope with their own response to Bethany's death, the school counselor had invited them to make paper snowflakes and glue them onto light blue envelopes made of construction paper. The final projects were laminated. The children were encouraged to write their remembrances of Bethany on a sheet of paper and put it into the envelope they had made.

We were invited to a ceremony in which the students unveiled a small metal marker dedicating the tree to Bethany's memory. I remember standing there with my arm in a sling, holding on to Jan and still very much in pain as we heard the counselor talk to the children and invite them to hang their snowflakes on the tree. Later, the snowflakes were collected and given to us so we could read the children's memories of Bethany. I was surprised at how many of them remembered her funny stories and jokes.

I had also wanted to mark the spot where Bethany died by putting a white cross on one of the pine trees near the place where our car came to rest. The road at that point runs through the Sand Hills State Forest, maintained by the state of South Carolina for forestry research. A friend made the cross for us, of sturdy 2-x-4-inch stock, and painted it white. I ordered blue vinyl lettering (Bethany's favorite color) to indicate her name, age, and the date of her death.

On April 18, the hearing for Darrell was held in the morning, and several of our good friends came down to support us. Afterward, we ate lunch together, then drove in a caravan to the tiny community of Middendorf, near the intersection of Highway 1 and "Widow Johnson Road." Not wanting to harm one of the Forest Service's trees, we nailed the cross to the weathered trunk of a dead tree near the spot where Bethany died.

Later, we planted a pine seedling from the site in our front yard, along with a Japanese "weeping" cherry tree and a blossoming cherry.

The wonderful people at Woodhaven had created a "Bethany fund" after her death, designed mainly as a vehicle for church members and friends to contribute to her funeral expenses. When there was money left over, we were invited to determine how it should be spent. Woodhaven had recently begun hand bell choirs for children, youth, and adults. Indeed, one of my last church-related memories of Bethany was a Christmas program in which she proudly rang her little bell as the children's hand bell choir performed.

Hand bells are very expensive, and we had begun the program with only two octaves. Jan and I used some of the "Bethany fund" money to buy additional bells, and the children's hand bell choir dubbed themselves "the Bethany Ringers." I never heard them play after that without crying.

Mark Burden, a dear friend, played in the adult hand bell choir. Sometime later, he and his wife Karen purchased a "B7" bell for the choir, because, he said, "Bethany will always be seven." The youth choir, many of whom were children when Bethany was in the hand bell choir, pitched in and bought us a "silent" B7 bell—one that has no clapper—as a reminder that her memory was still with us, though her voice had been silenced. It still adorns the mantle over our fireplace. We later contributed to the purchase of an additional octave of bells.

We also used remaining money from the Bethany fund, along with some of the insurance money we had received, to purchase furnishings for the first floor of the new building addition at Woodhaven, which would serve children and youth.

About the time Bethany died, nearby Campbell University, a fine Baptist college, was in the process of beginning a divinity school. Wanting to support the effort and also to remember Bethany, we, along with family members and friends, contributed funds to establish the "Bethany Rush Cartledge Scholarship." In this way we sought to remember Bethany and assist divinity school students at the same time.

We did not think of these memory-focused activities as morbid, but as concrete ways to remember Bethany while moving on with life. Moving on was not always easy, however. When one suffers a deep loss, there is an equally deep sense of loneliness because others do not share the same depth of grief.

I found myself resenting others who could go about their daily business as if nothing had happened, even if they never knew Bethany. For that matter, I was surprised to discover that I even felt offended by the arrival of spring. During a solitary walk through Hemlock Bluffs, a nearby park, I stood on an overlook and breathed in the warm air, the fragrance of new growth, the unmistakable signs of spring—and got mad. A bit of mental excavation helped me realize that I resented the new life that spring represented. "What's with all these blooming dogwoods and budding roses?" I asked. "Why does the breeze feel so warm?"

Somehow, I subconsciously expected the world to remain locked in winter, like my heart. I had to remind myself that people die every day. The world can't stop for every death, even the ones most precious to us. It didn't stop for Jesus, but Good Friday and Black Saturday gave way to Easter Sunday, and suddenly death was no longer the end.

It occurred to me that Bethany had left this world's winter for an eternal spring where she could go bare-footed every day. "Maybe now," I wrote in a free-verse reflection, "maybe this world's spring can shake my winter and thaw this mourning chill." But the sense of spring came and went.

Like Jan, I thought it wise to ask for help in working through my grief, so I sought counseling. A friend recommended a man who had written one of the leading textbooks on transactional analysis. He operated a small counseling center out of his home, deep in the woods outside of Chapel Hill, and I was comfortable talking with him.

In our sessions, we explored various issues related to what Jan and I were experiencing. He seemed to expect me to harbor more inner rage than I recognized, but I never really experienced the same kind of deep anger that Jan did. I was not pleased with what Darrell had done, but I felt little real hostility toward him for causing Bethany's death. I never believed that he intended to hurt our child, and I knew that he would always be haunted by what he had done. He was a young man lost in his own sorrows, prey to the inner demons that drove him to drink. Perhaps, since I felt some sense of culpability for my failure to avoid Darrell's careening truck, it was easier for me to feel some measure of compassion for him.

That is not to say I was not angry, but I felt more fury for the beer companies that continue to profit from fostering addiction than for a man who had fallen victim to their pitch. I knew he was responsible for Bethany's death, and I was justifiably angry about it, but I also felt sorry for him. In some ways, I considered him to be a victim, too.

Most of the immediate anger I felt at him arose from his attempt to avoid taking responsibility by asking for a trial. This caused us additional grief and cost us thousands of dollars, and we knew that he took the action intentionally. Even so, I could understand his desire to avoid going to jail by trusting the same lawyers who had gotten him off the hook before.

So when my counselor held up a big pillow and invited me to attack it with a foam bat, pretending it was Darrell, I couldn't put my heart into it. I was more concerned with understanding than with aggression, and the counselor wisely threw the pillow aside and let me talk. I later wrote a strongly-worded poem designed to express my feelings, with more satisfaction.

Counseling was helpful and the outside perspective was invaluable, but I still found more comfort in writing than in any other personal exercise. Writing free verse offered me a channel to express hurt and hope, a way to mark memorable moments in a lasting way.

For example, Memorial Day was unexpectedly difficult. I knew the holiday originated as a time to remember soldiers who died in wartime, but I could remember only Bethany. We received a copy of her school yearbook as Memorial Day approached. We were pleased, but also pained, to see a memorial page dedicated to Bethany. I expressed my feelings like this:

Memorial Day

Memorial Day.
Memory Day.
Bethany Day
  like every day
  without her.

Memorial marker.
Memorial page.
Bethany's marker.
Bethany's page.
  It shouldn't be!
Other parents adorn their cars with
  bumper stickers for honor students.
I need one that says
  "I have a child on the memorial page
    of the West Lake yearbook."
I thought it would hurt less by now.
  Less often,
  or less profound,
but grief is relentless,
  even when the shock has passed.
Every reminder is a hammer.
I'm beginning to understand
that she's not coming back.
  Ever.
  Not in this life.

All the messages I seek
   and coincidences I look for
   won't change it.

She's gone,
   except from our hearts
   except from our hopes
   except from our memories.
Remembering hurts like a bed of nails
   and yet I don't want to get up.
I don't want to forget
I don't want to let go
I don't want to lose sight
   of Bethany.
Memorial Day.
Memory Day.
Bethany Day
   is every day.
Still.
Until?

Father's Day, naturally, was even worse. One thing people must learn to expect when they lose someone dear is that the first year will be hell. I don't know a better way to describe it. Every special day, experienced for the first time in a new way, brings its own heartache. Jan and I learned to anticipate it. Sometimes the days of dread leading up to one of those special days would turn out to be worse than the day itself. But those days and the emotions they brought could not be avoided.

I thought it best to confront them head on. So, instead of trying to just get through the day as if it meant nothing special, I would devote focused time to thinking about Bethany and the particular way I was affected by her memories on that day. Sometimes I would express those feelings in writing. This was my way of emotionally venting. Afterward, I could move on.

Some attempts were more successful than others. On Father's Day, for example, I drew a blank. I was overwhelmed with memories and feelings, but couldn't get them out.

The July 4 holiday brought reminders of past playtimes, hot dog picnics, and glittering sparklers. Somehow, every new sound of celebration or burst of fireworks reminded me that I didn't feel like celebrating, that six months after the fact, the pain could still feel as raw as it did in the first few weeks.

This was a surprise to me, because there were many days when I felt as if we were making good progress. I would feel strong and confident, Jan would go about her work, and the days would seem almost normal. Then, out of the blue, either of us might wake up feeling as if the ceiling had caved in.

As I mentioned earlier, Jan and I learned that the progression of grief is not linear, but cyclical. As seminary graduates who had taken courses in pastoral care, we were both familiar with Elisabeth Kübler-Ross's "stages of grief," which she proposed for someone who had been told they had a terminal illness. The stages she described have been widely adapted as a model for how people experience grief in other settings as well. So we fully expected to experience denial, anger, bargaining, and depression on the road to acceptance. What we didn't expect is that, having thought we had arrived at acceptance, we would sometimes find ourselves back at the beginning, caught up in the jagged pain of loss.

In one poem I described the feeling as having had a "Bethanectomy," without anesthesia. The story was slightly different a couple of months later, as I sat on the front steps and watched Bethany's friends catch the bus for school. The sense of loss was still nagging and deep, accompanied by fantasies of a message from the beyond, yet leavened by the hope that while Bethany was not with us, she still *was*—

just in another place,
maybe another time,
wherever it is that God is,
where students learn their final lessons,
and do their eternal homework.

As we sought to give some shape to our concern about the problem of alcohol or drug-impaired driving, Jan and I joined the local chapter of Mothers Against Drunk Driving. As Jan will relate later, this gave us the opportunity to travel to Pittsburgh for a conference in early December, nearly eleven months after Bethany's death.

I will leave it for Jan to describe the meeting, the many victims we encountered, and the lasting effect the experience had on us. What I prefer to remember about Pittsburgh is the unforgettable opportunity we had to visit with Fred Rogers in his homey office above the public television studio where *Mr. Rogers' Neighborhood* was filmed.

Our relationship with Mr. Rogers began as it did for most people, sitting with our children and watching him on television. When we lived in Boone, *Mr. Rogers' Neighborhoo*d came on about the same time I usually arrived home from work in the late afternoon. I enjoyed sitting with Bethany while we watched and discussed the program.

We both loved Mr. Rogers' warmth, acceptance, and his desire to help every child appreciate just how special he or she is. We took particular delight in his visits to see how real people made crayons, musical instruments, or cakes. I thought Bethany had a healthy blend of both humility and self-esteem in her life, and I credited at least some of that to her exposure to Mr. Rogers.

In the weeks after I returned home from the hospital, Jan labored over countless thank-you cards for the many people who had expressed their love and sympathy, and I typed letters to people who may not have been nearby, but who had been important to Bethany in various ways.

One of those letters was addressed to Mr. Rogers. Though he had no way of knowing us, I simply wrote to thank him for being a part of Bethany's neighborhood, for making her feel special. I thanked him for helping her understand different feelings and appropriate ways to express them.

About a week later, the telephone rang. Jan answered it and immediately began to cry. "It's Mr. Rogers!" she blubbered. Mr. Rogers talked with Jan for fifteen minutes or so, then asked to speak to me.

He sounded just like he does on television. Warm, kind, understanding, and considerate. The first thing he did was ask if it was okay to call me by my first name, and he invited me to do the same. Fred expressed his sense of heartbreak for us and asked me to tell him more about what happened, how we were feeling, what we were doing. He was so kind, so pastoral, so *present* in that conversation, even by long distance. I wished I could be more like him.

I recalled a program in which Fred talked about how he often expressed his feelings through music, and told him that I had found poetry to be a good outlet for my own feelings. He encouraged me to send him copies of what I had written, gave us his address and phone number, and asked us to stay in touch.

We did. I would periodically send Fred a packet of things that Jan or I had written—usually poems, sermons, or articles that dealt in some way with Bethany and how we were dealing with her death. Inevitably, he would write back—always in a bold flowing script, always with a teal-colored Flair pen—and he would tell us how much he liked the writing, how wonderful he thought Bethany must have been, how special he thought Jan and I were.

When we began making plans for the MADD conference in Pittsburgh, I called to see if we could come by and visit with him in person. He graciously invited us to do so and gave careful directions to the studio.

When we arrived, I expected the receptionist simply to direct us to his office, but she knew Fred better than we did. She called to tell him we had arrived, and he came downstairs to meet us—not in his trademark cardigan with a shirt and tie, but in a neat blazer and turtleneck. I was surprised at how physically small he was, but he was never taller in my eyes than when he held out his arms to hug each of us in turn, and then led us up to his office. Along the way, he introduced us to everyone we met, giving equal importance to those who answered the phone and those who appeared on camera.

Fred freely gave us an hour or more of his time, patiently answering our many questions about his life and work, but clearly more concerned with learning about us and hearing our stories. Later, I tried to describe what it was like to sit and chat with Mr. Rogers himself:

Mr. Rogers' Office

Mr. Rogers' office is as snug as a hug,
comfortable like a well-worn sneaker,
cluttered like Santa's workshop.
There's no room for distance,
no desk to come between you,
just cozy chairs and close conversation—
a teddy bear's den made mostly
for listening.
The walls are covered in pictures and plaques
and nothing pretentious among them;
a Hebrew passage speaks of love,
and a Greek word heralds "grace"—
a giant piece of Chinese calligraphy adds something like
"If you wish to see yourself clearly,
don't look in muddy water."
There's nothing muddy here,

and perhaps reflecting back the essential you
is what Mr. Rogers does best,
*   for when he says "You are special,"*
*   you come to believe it just might be true—*
*   it must be true—*
*   Mr. Rogers wouldn't lie to you.*
The most beautiful thing about this neighborhood
*   is not just the warmth and the caring*

*   but that, when you go,*
*   you take some of it with you.*

I shall ever be grateful for the time and attention Mr. Rogers gave to us, and for the lessons our visit taught me. He could have had an assistant send us a sympathy card when he first got my letter, but he went out of his way to minister to us. So began a friendship that lasted until his death in early 2003, just a few months after he had sent me a thank-you note for the copy of my *1 & 2 Samuel* commentary I had sent him. "BRAVO!" he said, but it is Mr. Rogers who deserves the cheers. My lasting hero is not a mighty warrior or powerful statesman, but the gentle man from Pittsburgh who believed every person was unique and helped them believe in themselves.

✳

Jan

Darrell's sentence to twelve years in prison did not make the pain go away, though I did feel some sense of relief. I was relieved that the hearings were over and that he was serving time in prison. I found myself imagining what life was like for him in prison. I still harbored a great deal of anger and wished bad things were happening to him. I hoped he was suffering for the awful thing he had done to Bethany and our family. I fantasized about what I would do or say if ever put in a room alone with him.

I watched as he was taken out of the courtroom in handcuffs, feeling that he had received exactly what he deserved. He was paying the price for his actions and would now suffer consequences for the terrible choices he had made. But no amount of suffering he could experience and no amount of wishing him harm would ever bring Bethany back.

I came to realize that all my vengeful fantasies and delight in his imprisonment were eating away at me inside. I was becoming an angry and bitter person. Though I might not have exhibited such feelings on the outside, I was consumed with them on the inside. I did not like the person I was becoming and knew that I could not continue to harbor the thoughts that had found a home in my head and heart.

In my heart, I knew that one day I would have to forgive this man for killing my daughter. I just wasn't ready to make such an offer to him. People would occasionally ask if I had forgiven Darrell and I had no answer for them. I could only respond, "How do you forgive someone who kills your only daughter?"

I struggled through the summer months of 1994, seeming to just go through the motions of doing my work at the church. The youth calendar was full of summer events, but I did not really want to participate in any of them, much less lead them. My heart was not in my work or ministry. It took a tremendous amount of energy just to get through each day, especially on weekend retreats or weeklong events. I felt stuck in time. The lives of those around me had moved forward. Life had returned to normal for everyone else. I was still operating on Bethany time.

In early October of that year, Tony and I took a brief getaway to New York City. We ate in Chinatown, watched Broadway plays, and walked the streets. It was also a bittersweet time, as reminders of a previous visit to the city filled my mind.

In fall 1993, Bethany had accompanied us to New York for a weekend mission trip. During a time of sightseeing in Manhattan, we had taken her to see St. Patrick's Cathedral. She was impressed with the grandeur of the sanctuary, but seemed more interested in the prayer candles located along the walls of the church. She was curious about their purpose. We explained to her that people would light a candle and then say a prayer for someone in need. She asked if she could say a prayer and light a candle for her friend Christopher, who was then going through a difficult time. She lit the candle, and we prayed. It was a precious moment.

It seemed fitting that Tony and I visit St. Patrick's on this trip without her. We lit candles in memory of Bethany and prayed together in the same place that Bethany had prayed for Christopher and his family. I sensed her presence with me that day in a way that I had not felt since her death. The trip was a bright spot in the year, but it was not enough to reverse a gradually downward emotional slide.

The month of November would find me struggling to face each day. I knew that I was experiencing some symptoms of depression and had been since the summer months, but I did not want to admit it to anyone. I was spending a lot of time sleeping, preferring to stay in bed each morning rather than get up and face the day. I wasn't eating much. I didn't want to participate in my normal activities or spend time with friends. I felt sad and empty. I had little energy for work, relationships, and ministry.

All of these feelings came to a head on a Wednesday evening during a youth group meeting. I was doing my best to hold myself together enough to get through the session. The youth were being unusually rowdy that night, very inattentive and disruptive. As I tried to maintain control of the group, my patience was running thin.

Despite my best efforts, the youth were not cooperating and my efforts seemed in vain. I could not bear it any longer. I walked out of the room and onto the deck connected to the mobile unit in which we were meeting. I leaned on the deck railing, hung my head, and began crying. The youth remained in the room, uncertain of what to do or say to me. A church member happened upon me and I told her I just couldn't continue to go on like this. I gathered my belongings and went home to the couch.

Since Bethany's death, I had not really had any time off from work. Though we had been granted the leave of absence, I never completely unplugged from church responsibilities. Tony benefited much more from the leave than I did, as he recovered from his injuries—with me to look after him. I had found little time to rest, to relax, or to process what I was going through without still having to meet many other demands that needed my time and attention.

The previous ten months had left me feeling completely drained. I simply had nothing left to give to anyone. I left the church that evening and went home in a fog, feeling utterly defeated. Tony found me lying on the couch when he arrived home later. I told him that I just didn't think I could go back to the church for a while. I was depleted of energy and focus, and I wanted some time off. Tony consulted with the personnel committee, and we arranged for me to take a three-month unpaid leave of absence from my ministry responsibilities at Woodhaven.

It was during this time off that I finally decided to seek additional help for the depression I was experiencing. I went to my doctor and began a regimen of medication that enabled me to slowly return to my normal routines. I also continued seeing my counselor on a weekly basis. The time off allowed me to regain some strength and energy. It was also a time of reflection and regrouping. Realizing that I had been trying to do all and be all to all people, I learned to set limits for myself. The time off from the church was a gift that proved beneficial to my health and healing.

Tony and I had decided earlier to get involved with the local chapter of MADD. It was a way for us to channel some of our grief and anger into something good. It was also our desire to bring hope to others through our own experiences of grief and loss.

I was especially glad to find support from a group of people who had a good measure of experience and knowledge of the path I was walking. A drunken driver had affected many of the people who attended the Wake County MADD meetings. A few had been injured in crashes and lived to tell about it, but most had experienced the death of a loved one due to a drunken driver. Through my involvement, I saw that others had lived through their loss and grief. It gave me great hope. Involvement with MADD also gave me a place to share my story in hopes that it would make a difference in the life of someone else. As a MADD member, I also learned that I didn't want to live as a victim.

In December 1994, Tony and I were chosen to serve as the North Carolina representatives at the annual convention and candlelight vigil sponsored by the national MADD organization. The gathering was held in Pittsburgh, Pennsylvania, and we were honored and humbled to serve as representatives for our state. We were doubly excited because the trip gave us an opportunity to visit with Fred Rogers, as Tony has already described.

Since we had never attended an event such as this, we went not knowing what to expect. We anticipated a time of encouragement and mutual support, and we did come away from the experience with a renewed sense of survival and hope, but it did not happen in the way we expected.

The meeting included both joint sessions and a variety of seminars that covered specific topics related to loss and grief. I chose to attend a session just for mothers who had lost children to drunken drivers, while Tony attended a similar session designed just for fathers. Though we attended separate sessions, we had virtually the same experience and reacted to it in the same way.

As we participated in the weekend event, we witnessed many parents and family members who were stuck in their grief. Many of the individuals had experienced the death of a loved one many years ago. Some of them were still carrying and cradling 8-x-10-inch photos of their loved ones. They had been unable to move forward, and we saw in them a sense of hopelessness. They appeared to be stuck in the past and living as victims of the tragedy that had befallen them.

Back in our hotel room that evening, Tony and I talked about what we had experienced in our seminars. We both noted the sadness of those still carrying around large photos of their loved ones as much as ten years or more after their deaths.

Even with the knowledge that each person grieves in his or her own way, we made a vow to each other that night that we would choose a different path in our journey. We could fathom the deep sense of loss these people felt, but we could not imagine displaying our grief in such a way years from now. The weekend was a turning point for both of us. We did not know where our journey through grief would take us, but we were certain that we would find the most hope-filled path to survival and recovery.

We would not live as victims, defining our identity by the losses we had suffered. We would not be victims, but survivors—and not only survivors, but transformers as well. Together we made a decision that we would not only survive the horrible tragedy that had befallen us, but would also find ways to use what we had learned to help others who were experiencing the same kind of loss and pain.

That is a commitment we have kept. We felt that we owed it to Bethany, to ourselves, and to God to become good stewards of our pain. We did not want Bethany's death to be for naught. Because of that, Bethany's life and even her death take on meaning not only for us, but also for those who hear our story . . . even for those who are reading this book.

We returned from Pittsburgh to confront the Christmas season. For the first time in our lives, we dreaded the coming of Christmas. We did not want to face our first Christmas without Bethany alone, so we didn't.

It had been our tradition to have an open house for the Woodhaven family of faith during the holiday season. Despite the fact that I was taking a leave of absence from work, we decided to go on with hosting the event, though with a twist. We invited the church members to come and help us decorate our Christmas tree, something we did not want to do in a quiet house filled only with Bethany's absence. As our friends arrived at our home, each one chose an ornament from our collection and placed it on the tree. Many of them brought special ornaments as gifts. Our collection of angels, stars, and teddy bear ornaments grew substantially.

The first Christmas without Bethany was difficult and sad, and nothing could make it otherwise. My family had a tradition of gathering at my mother's home on Christmas Eve. Tony and I arrived at the appointed time, and my mother greeted us at the door. My brother Ben, his wife Carole, and their children, Benjamin and Kendall, also greeted us. I immediately began to cry. The reality of Bethany's absence was as pervasive as the Christmas greenery as our family gathered for the holiday.

Throughout the evening, I was very aware of the hole that Bethany's death had left in our hearts and our daily lives. I knew our family would forever be changed.

The reality of the hole in our lives became even clearer for me when we traveled to Georgia on Christmas Day to be with Tony's family, stopping on the way to leave a poinsettia beneath the roadside cross that marked the place where Bethany died.

Tony has two brothers, both of whom are married, with two children each. Everyone gathers at his parents' home to share a huge evening meal on Christmas Day, followed by a time of gift giving. It is the good tradition at their house that, after the presents are opened, we have all the grandchildren pose for a group picture. As Grant, Laura, Kristen, and Ashton posed this time, the picture was not complete. One child was missing, leaving a large empty space. I had to leave the room. It was another reminder that Bethany was no longer with us.

We received many caring gifts that year, both material presents and in the gift of presence. With the support of friends, we finally cleaned out Bethany's room. On New Year's Eve, we disassembled her beloved bunk beds and put them back together in Randy and Jill Keel's home. Bethany had been a frequent visitor in their home as she played with their daughter Molly. Sons Adam and Sam were a few years younger. Seven months after Bethany died, their son Seth was born, and I "adopted" him, taking joy in the new life and hope he brought into the world, even as Bethany had departed from our world.

As Seth grew old enough to move out of his parents' room, Adam and Sam would need to share a room, and the bunk beds would fit it perfectly. It was hard for us to take the beds from Bethany's room, but we knew they were no longer needed in our home. We were glad that other children who knew her would be able to use them.

Seth would never know Bethany, but he would bring much healing and hope to Bethany's mother. Jill and Randy knew that even with Bethany gone, we still wanted to have children visit our home and spend time with us. They were gracious enough to ask me to keep Seth on many occasions. Jill's sister Jo died two weeks after Seth was born, and I spent time caring for Seth during those hard days. I found it healing to my soul to cuddle

Seth in my arms, much the way I had done with Bethany. He was a gift, not only to his parents, but also to a mother who was missing the embrace of her own child.

One of the best Christmas gifts we received came in the form of a vacation. A generous and caring couple in our church offered us the choice of a week in Paris, London, or Hawaii, with all airline and hotel expenses covered. I was not keen on flying to Europe, so we chose to go to Hawaii. Thoughts of a tropical paradise sounded wonderful to us during the cold and barren winter season.

With the first anniversary of Bethany's death approaching, we chose to begin our trip the week before. We split our time between a beachfront hotel in Waikiki and an oceanside resort on the island of Maui. We were surprised on arrival to find a huge, beautiful bouquet of tropical flowers waiting in our room. Dear friends from Woodhaven had sent them for us. Even today, thinking of the adventures we had in carrying those flowers from one island to the next still brings a smile.

We made the most of our time in Hawaii, though little of it was spent dozing on the beach. We drove all over both islands, went snorkeling near Honolulu, and took a "whale-watching" boat trip off the coast of Maui. We also flew to the Big Island one morning, rented a purple convertible in Hilo, and drove south to visit the active Kilauea volcano before returning that evening.

We returned from our vacation refreshed, having experienced a wonderful gift. It was truly a time of rest and enjoyment for us, a high note on which to conclude the worst year of our lives. The road had been long and dark, but we had survived, and we were thankful to be alive with much of our lives still ahead of us.

chapter eight

From "What If?" to "What Now?"

Tony

As the second year of life after Bethany dawned, we were miles ahead of where we had been the year before, but we were far from home. I resonated with the way Robert Frost had closed his poem "Stopping by the Woods on a Snowy Evening." Progress had come in fits and starts, but there were still "miles to go before I sleep, miles to go before I sleep." We slept, of course, but our hearts were not yet at rest.

Some readers may have wondered why we have not said more about taking comfort in God or finding solace in prayer. Doesn't the old gospel song say, "Take your burden to the Lord, and leave it there"?

Speaking for myself, it is true that I sought comfort in the promises of God regarding the hope of heaven and the promise of the Spirit's presence. But my prayer life fell off the edge of the world, it seemed, and it remains a far different kind of encounter than I had known before.

This may sound strange, coming from someone who was an active pastor for twenty-six years, and who has continued in religious work, preaching often, for another six years and counting. Shouldn't pastors encourage people to pray, to seek God's favor, to ask for His comfort?

That is what one would expect. But after Bethany died, I suddenly found it very hard to ask God for anything. I still prayed, especially in my pastoral role, where I interceded with God for those who were in my spiritual family. But in my private prayer life, I stopped asking God for much of anything. I had prayed many times for Bethany, had prayed for her health, happiness, and safety, but God sent no angel to push the drunk driver's truck aside or to surround Bethany with a protective bubble. I had not really expected special treatment, but still I found myself angry with God for letting it happen. I wasn't about to ask God for anything else.

In time, my petulance with God gave way to clearer thinking, but I remained disinclined to ask for much. I studied the model prayer that Jesus taught when the disciples asked, "teach us to pray" (Matt 6:9-13; Luke 11:2-4), and began to look at prayer in a new way.

Jesus taught his disciples to ask for deliverance from evil, but not necessarily from harm. He taught them to pray for forgiveness—on the condition that they were willing to forgive others. The only request for physical or material blessing Jesus seemed to endorse was for daily bread, a basic necessity of life.

Even those limited requests in the Lord's Prayer are subsidiary to the first one: "your kingdom come, your will be done on earth as it is in heaven." Prayer, I came to believe, is primarily about posture—the posture we hold before God, whether our prayer bows to God's will or seeks our own. The truth is, much of what passes for praying in our world is really an exercise in "gimme-ism," but that is not what Jesus taught.

The Gospels record several instances in which Jesus encouraged his followers to ask for things (Matt 7:7-11 [=Luke 11:9-13]; 21:22; John 14:13-14; 15:7, 16; 16:24, 26). As a rule, however, those instructions are couched in one of two conditions: the believer is to pray for something so that God may be glorified, or to pray in Jesus' name.

I've heard both preachers and laypeople claim verses like John 14:14 as a license to ask God for anything: "if ye shall ask anything in my name, I will do it" (KJV). But that is no *carte blanche* invitation to ask for whatever we want because we know the secret words. When Jesus said "if you shall ask anything *in my name*," He was not teaching a magic formula for getting what you want. He was teaching that all prayer should be asked in His name, and that means to pray within the context of Jesus' will, as if He Himself were making the request.

Jesus set out the same sort of guideline for prayer in John 15:7, though in a slightly different way. In the context of talking about himself as the "vine," with believers as the "branches" who need to "abide in" the vine to have life, Jesus said, "If you abide in me, and my words abide in you, ask for whatever you wish, and it will be done for you."

The invitation to ask "for whatever you wish" and the promise that "it will be done for you" is prefaced by the condition "if you abide in me, and my words abide in you." If we truly find our life in Christ, earnestly seeking

His direction for our lives, then we will pray for what God wants, not what *we* want.

When I began to see this truth more clearly, I stopped asking for much in the way of personal requests, and when I did pray for something, I was more careful to add, "if it be your will." My private prayers became less colorful and more straightforward, involving less talking and more listening. For the most part, they consisted of some variation of the following: "Lord, here I am before you. You are God, and I am not. I'm grateful for all you have done for me, all you have given. Please forgive me of my shortcomings, even as I seek to forgive others. Now, if you're talking, I'm listening."

But God rarely spoke, at least in ways I could comprehend. Perhaps He knew how much anger I harbored toward Him, how disappointed I was that He had allowed Bethany to die. In time, I made peace with God over that. I got past the anger and remembered that, contrary to popular belief, God has not promised perfect protection to those who follow Him. If He did, then anyone would be a fool not to choose God's way, but everyone would be following for the wrong reasons.

God calls us to follow Him without conditions, without promises. If anything, the Bible teaches that those who follow Jesus open their lives to greater persecution and sorrow. Our only promise of security is for the next life, not for this one.

There have been times, I confess, when I wondered if God really exists. I still do. No amount of apologetics can prove the existence of God, though many things point to the divine reality. I cannot prove God, but I hope in God. I hope in God so strongly that I am willing to stake my life on the truth of that hope. I sometimes tell people that my definition of "faith" is "hope with feet on it."

I was feeling some of this when I wrote a poem about God and one of Bethany's favorite teddy bears that I kept in the car and sometimes cradled in my lap as I drove. I wondered why I sometimes seemed to get more comfort from stroking that teddy bear that Bethany had loved than I got from God. I longed for God to touch me with a sense of His power or show me a vision of Bethany safe and happy.

But I also wondered—if God were to touch me, could I bear His glory? If God granted me a vision of Bethany amid the wonders of heaven, could I still find beauty on earth? If God gave me answers for every question, would there be any place for faith?

For now, I realized, the grace of God could be found in many less visionary ways: in the embrace of His people, in the marvels of His world, in the hope of His future. I came to see even that little teddy bear as a soft and furry bit of grace, perhaps as much of God's touch as I could bear.

In ways such as this I found comfort in God, but I still felt far behind the curve when it came to spiritual leadership. That was why I had written an article in our church newsletter a few months before, inviting our people to move on in their spiritual growth and congregational excitement, rather than waiting for me to lead them onto higher ground.

It was an exciting time at Woodhaven. We were growing steadily. A second building project was rapidly drawing to completion. Our people were pumped up with possibilities and anxious to explore all that God had in store for them. I didn't want to hold them back and wasn't ready to quit, but I also didn't feel that I could keep up with them.

I remembered a period in my college years when I served as a summer missionary in Elijah Clarke State Park, near my home in Georgia. At least once per week, I would lead children on a hike along a nature trail that wound through a mixed forest of hardwoods and pines near the lakeshore.

Knowing that I had a responsibility for the children's safety, I would always begin by counting heads and warning everyone to stay within sight of me. Invariably, a couple of rambunctious boys would be far out of sight before we had gone 100 yards down the twisting trail. I would yell for them and tell them to come back. Sometimes they did.

I explained to our people that Jan and I were both feeling like trail leaders who were lagging behind the pack. We wanted to remain on the journey, but we did not want to slow them down because we could not presently match their enthusiasm.

In essence, we tried to give our church friends the permission to go on ahead that I didn't want to give to my young hikers. They seemed to appreciate the gesture, and other leaders emerged to take up our slack and keep the church moving forward.

While the church marched on, we struggled with grief and held on to hope. Most days were good, but others had their dark moments, like the time I found Jan weeping by the sink, holding on with both hands, tears dripping into a drawer filled with the kind of junk that kitchens collect. I remembered it this way:

The Bad Taste of Medicine

Jan stands
  beside the sink,
  holding on with trembling hands,
struggling for balance amid the swirling tides of memory.
Head down,
  tears drip
  into an open drawer packed
with the kind of junk that kitchens collect.
Amid the string
  and tape and thread,
  and lost Band Aids and rubber bands,
there sits a plastic medicine spoon
  designed for kids, tinted blue
  but stained with pink from its last poor rinse
  after Bethany's last dose of ampicillin,
  her "bubble gum medicine," the kind she liked,
A flooding recall
  of sleepless nights and fevers fought,
  of motherlove and stubborn coughs,
  years of struggle brought to naught
by one unthinking driver,
by one binge-drinking driver.
Now cartoon plates
  and cups and spoons
sit on the shelf in solitude
or hide amid the multitude
  of things that gather in kitchen drawers,
just waiting for the light of day
  to spark a mother's memory.

Our journey toward healing progressed jaggedly onward, with more time spent looking forward than looking back. For me, if I grew appreciably, it was in my appreciation of hope.

We were given many opportunities to talk about our experience in losing Bethany, how we continued to deal with it, what we had learned from it. When talking to young people and adults alike, I always emphasized the practical importance of making good choices, because I didn't want anyone to choose a road that involved both alcohol and driving. But, when I turned to the theological underpinnings of clinging to faith in the light (or dark) of tragedy, I consistently majored on hope, because hope was getting me through.

Peter says that God, by His great mercy, has given to us "a new birth into a living hope through the resurrection of Jesus Christ from the dead" (1 Pet 1:3). It is this living hope that kept Jan and me going through days of emptiness and longing. It is this living hope that gave (and gives) us courage to face the future.

There have been times when I wondered, before I knew better, why Paul included "hope" in his triumvirate of signs indicating spiritual maturity (as in 1 Cor 13:13 and 1 Thess 1:3). On the surface, hope seems to be the weaker sister of the three, a preliminary stage on the road to faith, perhaps. Both hope and faith seemed to involve trusting in something unseen—one just seemed more certain than the other. I wasn't so sure that "hope" deserved the place Paul had given it. It seemed to me that "faith" and "love" said it all.

But what I came to learn is that hope may in fact be the strongest of the three. Why? *Because when faith falters, hope is all you have left.* No one can lose a child in senseless fashion without experiencing a crisis of faith. Hope may seem to be weaker than faith because it is less certain, but I came to see hope as something deeper and stronger, because it has more staying power. In our Christian pilgrimage, hope comes *before* faith blossoms, and hope may endure even *after* faith falters.

When I say "I have faith that this is true," what I really mean is that I'm absolutely convinced of this, I have experience with this, I have no doubts about it. I have had some experience, perhaps, of God's presence, and so I can say I have faith that Christ lives in me.

Now, there are other areas of life and eternity in which I have no experience, but they are of immeasurable importance. Since Bethany's death, thoughts of heaven and eternity became like that for me. But, even as I think about eternity, I cannot help but have bushels of questions and days of doubt. Is there *really* such a place as heaven? Where is it? Is Bethany *really* there, now? What is she doing? What is she thinking? Is she still conscious of what goes on here?

Hope is the light I hold against the darkness. I can identify with the man whose beloved son was sick and who sought Jesus' healing touch. He said, "If you can do anything, please take pity on us and help us." Jesus replied, "*If* you can? Everything is possible for him who believes." And the man replied with honesty, and faith, and hope, "Lord, I believe, help me overcome my unbelief!" (from Mark 9:17-27)

What shall we do when we want to believe so badly that it seems our life depends on it, but our faith falters, and we are plagued by nagging fears and unanswered questions? This is where hope comes in, where we learn what a gift it can be.

I have come to believe that you cannot fully appreciate the value of hope until you reach a point at which you cling to it, like a slender, gossamer thread, holding on for dear life because hope is all you have to keep your head above the waters of abject despair.

I want more than anything to be certain that Bethany is happily inhabiting heaven now, that she runs barefoot in the sun and enjoys new friends, and that she looks forward to seeing her mommy and daddy again. There is much about eternity that the Bible only hints at—there is much that I cannot know, but *oh, how I hope!* And with God's help, that hope which comes through Jesus Christ will continue to be enough.

I hope, I wish, I long for greater knowing. I have learned that the presence of questions does not necessarily imply the absence of faith. So I keep trusting and hoping in something bigger than humankind and better than this world.

Once, when Frederick Buechner was reflecting on the subject of hoping and wishing, he said, "Sometimes wishing is the wings the truth comes true on. Sometimes the truth is what sets us wishing for it." (*Wishful Thinking: A Theological ABC* [New York: Harper & Row, 1973], 96)

The presence of hope suggests that there is a power at work to create that hope, and to set our hearts wishing for all the promises of God. At least one psalmist knew that power. On a day of exceeding disquietude, the writer gave voice to an internal dialogue that speaks to those who face despair: "Why are you cast down, O my soul, and why are you disquieted within me? *Hope in God*; for I shall again praise him, my help and my God" (Ps 42:5; 42:11; 43:5, NRSV).

Through the crises and calamities of our lives, I learned never to stop wishing, never to stop hoping, because in this way, I will never stop believing. This is the power and the glory of hope.

That sense of hope was reinforced in fall 1995, when I traveled to Israel on a study tour. I remember being greatly disappointed that there were no sandy beaches around the Sea of Galilee. Irrigation projects have lowered the level of the huge lake and turned the once mighty Jordan River into a mere trickle. As a result, the Dead Sea is also disappearing.

The traditional sites marking Jesus' birth, death, and resurrection were also a letdown, as they are covered with slabs of marble beneath ancient churches, but I was prepared for that.

Other aspects of the trip made it more than worthwhile. I wept and prayed at the Western Wall, which once supported the temple in Jerusalem. It is customary to leave prayerful notes stuck in the crevices of the wall, so I wrote Bethany's name and a short prayer in Hebrew to leave there.

I was suitably impressed by the mountainous desert wastelands between Jerusalem and Jericho, and the stark cliffs off the western edge of the Dead Sea were breathtaking. I was thrilled with visits to archaeological sites in Caesarea, Megiddo, Sepphoris, Beth She'an, and Masada.

But the most meaningful moment for me came during a Sunday morning visit to what is now called El-Elezarah, the biblical village of Bethany, just outside of Jerusalem. In Hebrew, the name "Bethany" means "house of poverty." We chose the name for our daughter because we wanted a biblical name, we thought it was pretty, and we joked that she would probably put us in the poorhouse.

Some of Jesus' closest friends lived in Bethany: sisters Mary and Martha and their brother Lazarus. Jesus stayed in their home when he came to visit Jerusalem. It was there that Jesus called Lazarus to arise from the dead and come out of his tomb.

A steep and narrow stairway, cut into the stone, leads down into the traditional tomb of Lazarus. From a fairly large chamber, even narrower steps lead down into a dark, lower chamber with deep niches cut into the side walls, repositories for ancient bodies or bones. After everyone else had left and I was alone in the tomb, I reached deep into one of the dark niches and left behind a small laminated picture of Bethany. No doubt breaking several laws, I also scooped up a small amount of the soil in an empty film container to be put in small alabaster boxes as gifts for Jan and my mother.

As the village of Bethany was associated with the themes of love, family, and resurrection life, I found special comfort in being there, and when I climbed up the dark and narrow steps of the ancient tomb to meet the Sunday morning sunshine, there was new light in my heart as well.

The renewed hope that Jan and I experienced found expression in a variety of ways as we became more active in the life of our church and the larger Baptist community. We also gave ourselves permission to have more fun, to travel, and to enjoy the life we still had, even without Bethany.

Some time before, we had begun to talk about the possibility of having another child. I was forty-three years old as 1995 dawned, and Jan was thirty-seven. We felt that we still had much to give. We did not believe God was through with us as parents, but we also knew that starting a new family would be a major step.

There was no guarantee that we could have another child, of course, but we wanted to be sure that our motives were appropriate and that we were not just trying to mask our pain in losing Bethany by bringing another child into the world. That would not be fair to the child.

We sought to be sure that we wanted another child for his or her own sake, not just as a substitute for Bethany. We knew it would be important that we not try to make over a new child in Bethany's image, but let that child be his or her own special person.

I sought advice from my minister's support group, and they peppered me with questions to help me examine my motives, but were also encouraging. Jan and I also talked with our counselors about the decision, and with other friends. It was not an easy decision to make. We knew that several medical obstacles would have to be overcome, and we had some concerns about our age, but we eventually came to the conclusion that it was the right thing for us to do.

At this point, I'll defer to Jan, who will discuss some other things and then come back to our quest for another child.

✳

Jan

We returned from our vacation in Hawaii on Tuesday, January 17, 1995, the day before the one-year anniversary of Bethany's death day. To aid us in dealing with this difficult anniversary, thoughtful members of the Woodhaven congregation had planned a remembrance service to be held during the regular Wednesday evening program.

When we arrived, balloons were tied to the sanctuary chairs. We were presented with a book of letters and cards from children, youth, and adults of the church. Each had written stories describing their favorite memories of Bethany. There was time for remembering Bethany aloud and for reflecting together on the journey we had traveled together during the past year. I had written a song to mark the first anniversary of her death, and I sang it during this service. The words captured some of my feelings about Bethany and the short time we had together.

If Only for a While (Bethany's Song)

Every time a rainbow paints the sky,
I long to see the beauty in your eyes.
Every time I see a shooting star,
I can't help but wonder where you are.
How I long for your embrace
And the smile upon your face;
Every day I seem to miss you more.

But I'm so grateful that God blessed me
With such a lovely child;
And I'm so grateful that I had you
If only for a while.

Every time I play your favorite song,
I long to hear you singing clear and strong.
Every time I see a child at play,
I listen for your laughter through the day.
How I long for your embrace
And the smile upon your face;
I can only hold you in my heart.

But I'm so grateful that God blessed me
With such a lovely child;
And I'm so grateful that I had you,
If only for a while.

We only had Bethany for a while, but the seven short years were filled with joy, adventure, love and pride. We missed Bethany, and we missed being parents. We knew that we still had a lot of love within us to give to a child, and we did not feel that we were finished being parents in this life. And so, we began to talk in earnest about trying to have another child.

We struggled with this decision, questioning the possibility that we might just be trying to replace Bethany. We discussed our feelings, fears, and desires with my obstetrician/gynecologist as early as June 1994, especially as it related to medical decisions.

If we were to have another child, I would need surgery to reverse the tubal ligation I had two years after Bethany was born, because we had decided to be a one-child family. My doctor referred us to a specialist at

Duke University Medical Center. Andy Norman, a good friend and an excellent surgeon who had performed the tubal ligation in Boone, also knew the doctor at Duke and recommended him highly. If anyone could successfully perform the "tubal anastimosis" that would reconnect my fallopian tubes and perhaps make it possible for us to have another child, we believed he could.

We scheduled an appointment with the doctor at Duke in July 1994, and he reviewed my medical history. He told us he was confident that he could do the tubal reversal. Though the typical pregnancy success rate following this surgery was around 50 percent, he told us that his patients had a success rate of around 85 percent, and we were encouraged. After talking with us about the operation procedures, however, he bluntly asked us why we wanted to have another child.

We explained our reasoning to him, and he listened intently. I think he understood that we were not just trying to replace Bethany, but he wanted us to be absolutely certain before doing the surgery. He encouraged us to go home and wait for at least six months. He wanted us to get through our first year of grief and to be certain of our decision to have another child. He told us to call him back if and when we reached that decision.

We confided in only a few of our closest friends about our desire to have another child. Naturally, they advised for concern and caution, but also shared in our hopes. Our friend Steve Bolton, a member of Tony's support group, put the decision in clear perspective for us. In his careful, measured way, he said, "I think, if you don't try to have another child, you might look back one day and regret it. But if you do try, whether you have a child or not, you will probably never regret it." Those words of wisdom seemed to seal the decision for us.

We went back to see the surgeon at Duke, and the surgery was scheduled for January 31, 1995. We kept our plans rather quiet, though we were delighted that we could arrange for our friend Evelyn DeRoche to be present as nurse-anesthetist. I had hoped to have the surgery early in the morning at Duke hospital and return home later in the day.

As the operation progressed, however, the surgeon discovered and removed a large benign cyst from one of my ovaries. He performed a test and pronounced that the tubal reversal was a success, but due to the removal of the cyst, he wanted me to stay in the hospital overnight. We left the hospital the next morning with no guarantees of another child. But we had the assurance of having no regrets for our decision and hearts full of hope for the future.

By the end of summer 1995, however, we were still unsuccessful in getting pregnant, and getting older all the time. The doctor suggested that Tony should have some tests done. The results were not encouraging. He had a varicocele—a large clump of blood vessels—in one testicle. The extra blood flow led to a higher than normal temperature, inhibiting sperm production.

Surgery to repair the varicocele was set for the end of September, and by the middle of January 1996 (following a major ice storm that left us without power for several days), a home pregnancy test came up positive, and a visit to the doctor confirmed it. We were expecting! The due date was October 5, and the coming months were to be busy ones.

At the time of my pregnancy, I was feeling healthier and stronger. I was farther along in my grief journey. My time in counseling had helped me work through the depression, anger, and grief related to Bethany's death. Months before the pregnancy, I was able to stop taking medication for depression. A new level of energy and enthusiasm returned in many areas of my life. Healing continued to come in many forms.

During the first two years of my grief, I often wondered if I would ever be able to return to work and find joy in my ministry. I wondered if I would be able to find the necessary energy and level of excitement that I had before Bethany's death. I did not, however, want to use Bethany's death as an excuse. I did not want to quit working or living life to the fullest and place the blame on my child's death. Though I knew that I would never be the same person I was before Bethany's death, I was willing to forge ahead with renewed hope and direction.

I was still working part-time at Woodhaven. I was also employed as a contract worker with the Baptist State Convention of NC, serving as chairperson of the Youth Conference Planning Team. I had previously served as a member of this team for four years, assisting in the planning of four summer youth weeks at Caswell.

My first summer as chair was in 1996, right in the middle of my pregnancy. The four weeks I spent at Caswell were long and hot. I tired easily but took advantage of afternoon naps. It was a significant time of renewal, and I was filled with hopeful expectation that grew along with the child within me.

With the summer behind me, I turned to making preparations for the birth of the baby. Bethany's room had been cleaned and prepared as the nursery. Friends from Woodhaven hosted a baby shower for us in the middle of September. A full church calendar kept me busy right up until the arrival of labor pains on a Sunday evening, after I had worked a full day at church.

The labor pains intensified to the point that I asked Tony to take me to the hospital late Sunday evening. The nurses determined that I wasn't ready to be admitted, so they sent us back home. I tried to sleep, but the intermittent labor pains kept me awake most of the night. Around 6:30 AM the next morning, we made our way back to the hospital. This time they let me stay.

After several long hours of labor pains that were not eased by the administration of two failed epidurals, the doctor told us to decide if we wanted to continue pushing or have a caesarean section. The baby's head was in a strange position, and I could not continue pushing due to excruciating back pain. I voted for the C-section. At 2:30 PM on Monday, September 30, 1996, Samuel Haywood Cartledge entered the world and our hearts. We welcomed his birth with tears of joy, mingled with the memories of his sister's birth ten years before.

Tony began taking pictures of Samuel as the nurses went through their usual procedures for newborns. Tony then accompanied Samuel to the nursery and celebrated with our friends and family who were waiting to welcome Samuel to the world. After the doctor sewed me back together, I was taken to the recovery room. Once the nurses got me settled in this area, they left me alone.

I felt a wave of grief coming over me. Tears began to fall, and I started shaking uncontrollably. A kind nurse noticed and inquired about my tears. She held my hand and listened as I explained to her that Samuel's birth had reminded me of the birth of my first child ten years before. I asked her if Tony could come be with me for a few minutes. She made the call and Tony came and comforted me. The wave of grief had come very unexpectedly, a reminder of the cyclical nature of grief. Once I was moved from the recovery room, the grief gave way to feelings of joy as I held Samuel in my arms for the first time.

chapter nine

"All Things Work Together for Good"

Tony

Coping with loss is a day-to-day struggle. In the first months, it was more like hour-to-hour, even minute-to-minute. There were times when it was extremely difficult to think of anything other than the large empty spot Bethany had once occupied.

As months passed, however, I recognized a need to sublimate some of those desperate longings into more productive activity, channeling energy away from abject mourning and into other projects. To a degree, our work at church provided a helpful outlet for both Jan and me. We reengaged the work of ministry with as much heart as we could muster and found it to be both fulfilling and healing. For the most part, our church family remained sensitive, accepting the leadership we could offer and being patient when our energy level ran short.

Work was helpful, and sermon preparation offered a wonderful creative outlet for writing, but the nights were still there to face, and the early mornings. While writing was therapeutic for me, I came to realize that it would not be helpful to overindulge in the sometimes morose free verse that had brought me comfort in the first few months following Bethany's death.

So it was that the invitation to write a volume for a new Bible commentary series to be published by Smyth & Helwys came as a real gift, a positive challenge I could sink my teeth into. I had previously published a revision of my doctoral dissertation (*Vows in the Old Testament and the Ancient Near East*), but it was a scholarly treatise destined more for library bookshelves than for active desktops. I had wanted to do something more useful with my academic preparation.

I have read many biblical commentaries, but few that I considered to be both academically responsible and aesthetically readable. I liked the challenge of writing a commentary that remained in touch with good scholarship while also engaging the reader.

The series was still in the planning stage when Smyth & Helwys invited me to Atlanta for a small meeting with editors and other prospective writers. The process was so early, in fact, that I was invited to choose which Old Testament book or books I wanted to tackle.

Though I remain enthralled with the Hebrew Bible in all of its diversity, the choice was easy. I have always been enamored with the historical narratives, especially the stories of how Samuel, Saul, and David led Israel to move beyond traditional tribalism to the beginnings of a nation.

So, I asked for 1–2 Samuel. I knew it would be a huge project, but I was undeterred—I knew there would be enjoyable work to fill any sleepless nights or early mornings for the next several years.

In the years since, I have wondered if I may have subconsciously chosen 1–2 Samuel because the theme of death is fairly prominent, especially in David's life. David was well acquainted with death—most commonly someone else's, and at his hands. When all others despaired, young David slew the giant Goliath, according to 1 Samuel 17, and from that day he gained fame as a walking weapon of mass destruction.

David was so successful in later battles with the Philistines that the women would cheer, "Saul has slain his thousands, and David his ten thousands!" (1 Sam 18:7). Saul once tried to engineer David's death by sending him on an errand to return with one hundred Philistine foreskins, knowing that David would have to kill to collect them, or be killed in the process. David returned with not one hundred, but two hundred.

But David's familiarity with death did not make the loss of loved ones any easier. When he learned that both Saul and his close friend Jonathan had been killed in battle, David's lament (2 Sam 1:19-27) was a model of grief, especially with respect to Jonathan:

> How the mighty have fallen in the midst of the battle!
> Jonathan lies slain upon your high places.
> I am distressed for you, my brother Jonathan;
> greatly beloved were you to me;
> your love to me was wonderful,

passing the love of women.
How the mighty have fallen,
and the weapons of war perished! (2 Sam 1:25-27)

This was the first of several significant deaths that David faced. In a moment of weakness, David instigated a sexual liaison with Bathsheba, the wife of one of his most faithful soldiers, and she became pregnant. David recalled Bathsheba's husband from battle, hoping he would sleep with his wife so the sin would go undetected. When Uriah refused, David callously ordered Joab to put the faithful soldier in the way of mortal danger (2 Sam 11).

The prophet Nathan declared to David that the sword would not depart from his house, and the remainder of 2 Samuel describes how David faced one painful death after another.

The child born to Bathsheba was the first, and David's approach to grief in the death of the young child is interesting. When the boy became ill, David fell into a period of abject grief and prayer, begging God to spare the child's life. He would not eat, sleep, bathe, or tend to the nation's business, but spent his days and nights in tears and prayer.

Once the child died, however, David washed his face, ate his food, and returned to the affairs of state. Others were puzzled that he did not join the public mourning for the child, but David had already poured out his grief. Once the child died and it became clear that his guilty prayers were of no avail, he put grief aside. Some may suggest that David was in denial, but it seems more likely that he was simply further along in dealing with his grief, and ready to move on.

The story of the young child's death (2 Sam 12) is followed by an account of fratricide between two of David's grown sons. Amnon, David's eldest, fell in lust with his half-sister Tamar. He tricked her, raped her, and left her to fend for herself. David was very angry, the text says, but took no action. Absalom, Tamar's full brother, was determined to avenge his sister, however. He bided his time for two years, then invited all of David's sons to a party where he got Amnon drunk and ordered his servants to murder him. Absalom then fled the country, in essence depriving David of two sons at once.

After hearing a false report that Absalom had killed all of his other sons, David "arose and tore his garments and lay on the earth. And all his servants who were standing by tore their garments" (2 Sam 13:31). Even after learning that Amnon alone was dead, David joined his other sons in expressing deep sorrow: "the king's sons came and lifted up their voice and wept. And the king also and all his servants wept very bitterly" (2 Sam 13:36).

The story goes on to say that, as Absalom fled the country, David "mourned for his son every day" (v. 37), but the ambiguous context leaves the reader to wonder if David was mourning for his dead son Amnon or his lost son Absalom.

These events propelled David into a downward spiral. Never again was he the great king who unified the peoples of Israel and Judah, leading them to establish a secure and growing homeland. From that point forward, David lost much of his leadership ability and did well to survive. In time, David allowed Absalom to return in peace, only to see the young man gather a following and lead a rebellion against him.

David chose to flee rather than to fight his son, though Absalom unwisely chose to lead an army of fellow mutineers into battle against David's forces. David ordered his soldiers to "deal gently for my sake with the young man Absalom," but Joab, his pragmatic military chief, ignored David's sentimental instructions. When Absalom fell into Joab's power deep in a forest, Joab and his men killed the rebel leader. To avoid bringing his body back to David, they threw Absalom into a pit and raised a large mound of stones over it.

David eventually heard the news, however, and responded with raw, conspicuous grief: "And the king was deeply moved and went up to the chamber over the gate and wept. And as he went, he said, 'O my son Absalom, my son, my son Absalom! Would I had died instead of you, O Absalom, my son, my son!'" (2 Sam 18:33 [Heb 19:1]).

David's grief was so intractable and so disheartening to his faithful soldiers that Joab forcefully pressed David to bring his weeping under control and pay appropriate honor to his troops, lest they desert him.

There is little evidence in the narrative that David made much progress in moving past this final blow. Though restored to the throne of Israel, he remained a broken man and died with a bitter spirit, seeking vengeance on those who had opposed him.

As I learned these things about David's grief journey, I felt an even stronger desire for a different outcome.

Our son Samuel, as we have mentioned before, was a part of that outcome. I mention him here because his name is directly related to the work I was doing. Samuel had been dreamed about, prepared for, conceived, carried, birthed, and raised through his first few years while I was working through 1–2 Samuel, writing a commentary that eventually totaled 747 published pages.

"Samuel" seemed to be a fitting name—not only because of the book, but also because of the story of his birth. The namesake of 1–2 Samuel was born at a time when his mother was distraught because she had no children. Hannah prayed earnestly for God to give her a child—even making a vow to return him to God if He should grant her a son. God heard and responded positively to her prayer: the name "Samuel" literally means "heard of God."

Jan and I felt that God had heard and responded to our prayers, too. We knew what it was to be distraught, what it was to pray for a child, and what it was to experience the joy of a new birth. Samuel was and is a gift who brings new joy to our lives and new hope to our hearts.

Before Samuel was born, we asked the doctor not to tell us if ultrasound examinations revealed the baby's gender—we wanted to be surprised. Secretly, I had hoped for a boy. I was afraid that a girl would be too subject to comparisons with Bethany, that we might subconsciously try to make her over in Bethany's image.

Samuel took care of that problem. He is clearly his own self, with his own personality. While there are occasional mannerisms that remind us of the sister he never knew but we still talk about, there is no danger that we will ever confuse the two.

As much as we have grieved Bethany's absence, we have celebrated Samuel's presence. We would never have chosen for Bethany to die, but neither can we imagine life without Samuel. Our prayers were indeed "heard of God," and we have been abundantly blessed.

*

Jan

Even in the midst of the joy and celebration surrounding Samuel's birth, we were still dealing with situations related to Darrell's prison term. Soon after the sentencing, we registered with the South Carolina Department of Corrections to ensure that we were contacted when he was screened for work release, community educational programs, furloughs, or transfer to another prison facility.

We also registered with the South Carolina Department of Probation, Parole, and Pardon office. This would grant us notification when Darrell was scheduled to appear before the parole board.

The programs worked better in theory than in practice. Darrell spent the first half of his prison term at the Lee Correctional Institution in Bishopville, South Carolina. He was screened for placement in a community work center in October 1994, having served only four months in prison. Our first notification was a letter indicating he had not been approved for the program. We also did not receive notification when he was granted a one-day leave in August 1996 to attend his mother's funeral.

Darrell's first parole hearing occurred in February 1997. In preparing to oppose his early release, we wrote letters to the parole board, stating the reasons for our opposition. Adults, teenagers, and children from Woodhaven also filled several file folders with letters of opposition. We also asked the governor of South Carolina and several senators and representatives of the state house to write letters on our behalf, and they kindly obliged.

The parole board meeting was held at the Broad River Correctional Institution in Columbia, South Carolina. Darrell and his family had the opportunity to speak to the board, stating their desire for an early release. Traveling to a meeting actually held on the prison grounds was not particularly appealing, but we thought it was important for us to be present, too. We wanted to put voices and faces on the letters already included in the permanent record.

After spending time in a waiting area, Tony and I were ushered into a medium-sized room where the board members sat at three sides of a long table, with one long side open to a row of chairs set up for those who made their appeals to the board. We thought about the many people who had sat there and their conflicting motives.

Tony and I explained that we did not feel Darrell had served enough of his sentence to justify early release. We emphasized that he had demonstrated little remorse for his actions. We did not feel that he had received the help he needed for his addiction to alcohol, and we requested that parole be denied.

After hearing from both families, the parole board met in closed session. We were then called back into the room and told that parole had been denied. The board thanked us for coming and expressed their sorrow for Bethany's death. We left feeling that our journey, though emotionally trying, had served a purpose.

In August 1997, we received a letter from Darrell's wife, Tiffany (whose name has also been changed out of consideration for her privacy), whom he had married during his incarceration. She expressed to us that Darrell was a good person, but that he had fallen into the bad habit of drinking with his working buddies. Again, the blame for his problems was placed on someone else.

Tiffany told us that Darrell was a responsible citizen when it came to working and supporting his family. She wrote that he had a kind heart and that he loved children. She wanted us to know that he was suffering as a result of his prison time and that he would continue to suffer upon parole.

Once released from prison, she said, Darrell would be thirty thousand dollars in debt for past child support payments, private school tuition for his daughter, and medical payments. He would not be able to obtain a driver's license for three years once paroled. She reminded us that he had lost years with his own daughter, who was seven years old at the time of the wreck. She expressed hope that we would one day find it in our hearts to forgive Darrell.

The letter did not have its intended effect. Rather, it infuriated me. I thought, "How dare she write and tell us about the suffering that Darrell was experiencing?" Did she not know that he had given Bethany a death sentence, and that we had received a life sentence? We would spend the rest of our lives missing our daughter as a direct result of Darrell's terrible choice to drink and drive. Had she had a lapse in memory? Did she not know that Darrell was sent to prison for a reason and he was reaping the consequences of his actions? Had she forgotten who the victims were in this case?

In a sense, we would agree that Darrell was the victim of a local judicial system and a family system that had failed to hold him accountable for his actions, but we thought the time for accountability had arrived. I responded to the letter and reminded Tiffany that Bethany, our family, and friends were the main victims in this case. I wrote of the suffering we had experienced as a result of Bethany's death. Did she realize we also had financial issues? We had to pay for Bethany's funeral and medical expenses related to Tony's injuries. We had to purchase a new car to replace the one that was destroyed in the wreck. We had spent money to hire legal assistance because Darrell had refused to acknowledge his guilt.

As I ended the letter, I suggested that the next letter we receive come from Darrell. We had not heard anything from him. He had not expressed any remorse to us beyond a bumbling "I'm sorry" when I confronted him on the day he asked for a trial, expanding and extending our heartache. I assured her that we would be willing to listen if he wanted to speak with us, either in person or by writing us a letter.

We soon received notice that Darrell was being screened for a labor crew work release program. Acceptance in this program would grant him a transfer to Palmer Pre-Release Center in Florence, South Carolina. He would be allowed to work off-campus under direct supervision at a state, county, or municipal agency.

Darrell was approved for the program and moved to the Palmer Center. We were gratified to learn that he was participating in Alcoholics Anonymous and was receiving counseling during his prison term. He seemed to be taking some of the necessary steps to bring about change in his life.

One of those steps included writing us a letter to express his remorse for his actions and the pain he had caused our family. The letter arrived in our mailbox ten days after I had sent my letter to his wife. In part, Darrell wrote,

I know what I did was wrong and it was nobody's fault but my own. I know I put your family through a terrible ordeal but I can only hope that you can one day find it in your hearts to forgive me for what I have done. There's not a day that goes by that I do not think about it, wishing it had never happened or wishing it had been me that lost a life instead of Bethany because, after all, I was the one that made the stupid, irresponsible choice of drinking and driving.

I hope you believe me when I say I am truly sorry for the pain and suffering that I have caused your family. I never meant to hurt anyone. I just wish there was something I could say or do to change the past but I know I cannot do so. I can only hope to make a difference in the future. Since I have been incarcerated I have been through alcohol and drug programs and Alcoholics Anonymous, sharing my story with other people, hoping to prevent someone else from making the same mistake that I did.

When I finished reading his letter, I felt some gratitude. I knew this was a huge step for him. It was also a risk, because he had no guarantee that we would extend any amount of forgiveness to him. I found myself feeling grateful that he was able to say the words "I'm sorry" and finally admit responsibility for his actions.

I had harbored much anger and bitterness toward Darrell for several years following Bethany's death. I hated what he had done to Bethany and to our family, and I was glad that he was sentenced to prison. I would often daydream about what I hoped was happening to him while he was serving his time. I wanted him to suffer and experience pain, thinking that if he were being punished for his deadly actions it would somehow make me feel better.

Now the next step was mine, but I was reluctant to take it. I put the letter away, not yet ready to respond to him. How do you forgive someone who killed your daughter? How do you offer forgiveness for such a horrible act? What would God have me do in this situation? The questions remained with me for another year.

I was participating in a women's support group at Woodhaven, and we were working through the book *Search for Significance* (Robert S. McGee, LifeWay Press). One chapter focused on forgiving others. As I worked through the companion daily exercises, I realized that I needed to forgive Darrell in order to rid myself of all the anger and bitterness I harbored. I realized that I did not need to do this just for Darrell. I needed to do it for myself.

I knew I could only find such forgiveness by looking at Darrell through God's eyes. Darrell and I were created by the same God, and we both were children of God. God didn't love me more than he did Darrell. When I began to see the man with God's eyes and heart, I knew I had to find forgiveness in my heart for him. My ability to extend grace and forgiveness to Darrell was related to the degree to which I had experienced grace and forgiveness through Jesus Christ. The scars of the cross were suffered for all, even for those who seem to deserve it least. I knew that forgiving Darrell was a necessary step in ridding myself of the anger and bitterness that had kept me from moving forward to healing.

In my quiet time one morning following a daily exercise in the *Search for Significance* workbook, I prayed this prayer:

God, I am being asked to do something that is very hard. I pray that you would help me this day to forgive as you do. You have forgiven me fully and completely and I want to do the same with those who have offended me, even those who seem to least deserve it. Today I forgive Darrell for killing Bethany. I can do this because of your forgiveness in my life. Though this doesn't excuse what Darrell did to me, I know that this is what I need to do to find the peace that passes all understanding. I want to release the anger and bitterness I have carried during the last four years. Thank you for the courage and strength that helps me to do what I once thought was impossible. Amen.

I then wrote Darrell a letter, offering him forgiveness for his actions and the pain he had brought to my family. I told him that I would always hold him responsible for the deadly choices he made but that I wanted to forgive him. I shared that God had forgiven me many times in the past and that

God also desired for me to forgive those who had hurt or offended me. I told Darrell that I hoped he would be able to forgive himself and that his future choices would bring goodness and hope to the world.

I do not have a copy of the letter I wrote to him to include here in these pages. I suppose that is symbolic of the full release of the anger that I experienced when I placed the letter in the mailbox. A heavy burden was lifted as I let go of the anger and Darrell.

From that moment to the writing of these words today, I do not harbor any ill feelings toward Darrell. I no longer feel the deep anger I once felt toward him. Forgiveness did not mean I could overlook his actions or deny the pain he brought to Bethany and our family. Forgiveness did not mean I was able to completely forget what he did. The scars will remain forever. In some ways, as long as we remember the hurt, forgiveness remains an ongoing process.

Forgiving Darrell enabled me to move forward to hope and healing in my own life. I was able to acknowledge that his actions had changed my life, but I would not let them destroy my life. Along the way, I have discovered that forgiveness is a growing thing, and it was a necessary step toward acceptance, hope, and healing.

I seldom think about Darrell these days. I don't know where he lives. I don't know where he works or how he spends his days. I don't know if he has forgiven himself. I only know that there is a deep sense of peace that has found residence in my heart since I placed a letter of forgiveness in the mailbox.

A second parole hearing was held in March 1998. The format and location of the meeting changed at this point. To participate, we would have to go to a designated correctional institution and communicate with the parole board via videoconferencing. We chose not to attend this hearing in person, but we did write letters of opposition to the parole board. Parole was again denied.

The third parole hearing was scheduled for April 1999. Conversations with South Carolina Department of Corrections personnel indicated that Darrell was nearing release. He had been a model prisoner, earning days of credit off of his sentence for good behavior. He was receiving counseling and had been through drug and alcohol rehabilitation programs. It appeared that he had done all that was necessary to earn an early release.

I did not feel strongly about attending this parole hearing. I suppose writing the letter of forgiveness to him had a lot to do with my level of interest in his fate at this time. I didn't feel motivated or interested in opposing his parole in person, so we sent a letter to the board, stating our willingness to accept whatever decision they rendered.

We had earlier been advised that Darrell would have more post-prison supervision if he were granted parole before his "max-out" date, which was scheduled for September 2001. If he stayed in prison until that time, there would be no probation requirements or conditions placed on him upon his release.

While we did not oppose Darrell's release, we asked the board to attach strictly enforced conditions to his parole. Namely, we encouraged the board to instruct him to refrain from using alcohol or illegal drugs, and from patronizing bars or other establishments whose primary business was the serving of alcohol. We requested that he be enrolled in and faithfully attend an ongoing program of alcohol/drug rehabilitation, such as Alcoholics Anonymous. We had been told that state law would prohibit him from obtaining a driver's license for three years following his release, but we asked the board to spell it out in the conditions of his parole.

The parole was granted, and Darrell was released from prison in April 1999, having served only four years and ten months of the twelve-year sentence. In a sense, his release from prison was freeing for me. It was the end of the emotional roller coaster that I had been on since Bethany's death and during Darrell's prison sentence. There would be no more phone calls to the SC Department of Corrections office to check on his status, no more appearances before the parole board, no more letters to write opposing his release. I had written the most important letter—a letter of forgiveness— and it was time to close that chapter of our lives and move forward.

I realized, however, that with the closing of one chapter, it was time to begin another one. I wanted to do something positive in an effort to share our story, hoping that it might make a difference for good in the lives of others. I wanted to do something tangible to keep Bethany's memory alive, an effort not to let her death be in vain. During the first year of our grief, we had made a commitment that we would share our story whenever we were given the opportunity. As mentioned previously, we had many opportunities to do so through newspaper and television interviews. Tony contributed elements of our story for inclusion in the book *When a Child Dies*. We wanted others to hear and learn from us.

Both of us have had opportunities to speak to various groups over the years. We have shared our story with youth in churches and high schools. We have spoken to college students during campus-wide alcohol awareness events. We have led seminars on dealing with grief and the death of a child.

Our goal has always been not only to share our story, but to encourage others to make positive choices for good and not for evil. We have tried to help others understand that the choices they make affect other people, sometimes in costly and deadly ways. We have encouraged young people to realize that the choices they make today will have a lasting impact on their lives. We have reminded them that their choices might even affect another innocent child and her family.

I have had the opportunity to speak on several occasions before committees of the North Carolina General Assembly, lobbying for the strengthening of drunken driving laws. I have shared our story with lawmakers in hopes of putting a face on the victims of this senseless crime. I wanted them to see Bethany's face and to hear her story with the hope that drunk drivers would be held accountable for their actions and other families would not suffer as we had.

North Carolina, like many other states, has made significant progress in getting repeat offenders off our highways. Laws have been passed that serve to lengthen jail time and to impound the vehicles of those caught driving while impaired. I find great satisfaction that our story has perhaps been a catalyst for change and the strengthening of drunken driving initiatives in North Carolina.

The U.S. Department of Transportation, in partnership with the Ad Council, started a national campaign using pictures of actual victims who were killed in drunken driving incidents. We were contacted by an ad agency in New York and willingly submitted photos and videos of Bethany to be used in the campaign.

Bethany was chosen as a "poster child" for the multimedia campaign. Ads were broadcast nationally through television commercials, radio spots, newspaper and magazine print ads, and roadside billboard public service advertisements. Even in death, Bethany was still able to touch the world with an important message.

Opportunities such as these proved to be a gateway to personal growth and healing. Each time I have the chance to share our story and my personal journey through grief, it is another step toward growth, healing, and hope. It is a hard story to tell, and sometimes the telling of it takes me back through painful memories. Despite this, I will continue to share the story and never lose hope that Bethany, even in death, can continue to make a difference in the lives of others.

chapter ten

The Road Goes Ever On and On

Tony

Bilbo, the inveterate hobbit who grew from J. R. R. Tolkien's prolific imagination, was no ordinary inhabitant of Hobbiton. Though he spent many years following the typical, quiet pattern of life expected of a good hobbit, Bilbo was chosen by the wizard Gandalf to accompany a dozen dwarves on a dangerous quest. Bilbo was hesitant to leave his comfortable hobbit hole, but reluctantly joined Gandalf and the dwarves on their adventure. Along the way, in a deep, dark cave, he discovered a ring that would ultimately change the fate of Middle Earth, which was on its way to becoming a whole new world.

Bilbo's newfound spirit of adventure made him a bit of a misfit back in Hobbiton, where stability was prized over all else. But Bilbo had learned that the world—and the future—was bigger than anything his fellow hobbits could imagine. As Bilbo composed his memoirs and took walks with his nephew, Frodo, he was prone to express his thoughts in song: "The road goes ever on and on . . . ."

And so it has been for Jan and me. We did not ask for the adventure that changed our lives and ushered us into a whole new world, but we have learned that the road goes on and on, with new turns every day.

We learn from where we have been, and we look forward to where we are going.

Five years after Bethany died, I used my personal column in the *Biblical Recorder* to reflect publicly on some of the lessons I had learned. I remembered her life: Bethany was bubbly and bouncy. She loved french fries, pizza, and hot dogs. She always wanted to ride a horse. She liked to tell corny jokes. She cared about others, especially when they were hurting. Bethany reminded me of the value of joy and love and appreciation for every moment of life.

Other lessons began when her life on earth came to an end. Jan and I learned that it really is possible to absorb a slashing wound to the heart and still survive, and still thrive.

The first year after Bethany's death was dark and empty and frightening. We lived with great holes in our hearts, with a constant nagging sense of incompleteness—but we got through.

The second year was also hard, but the pain was less and smiles were more frequent. By the third year it was easier to remember how Bethany blessed us without bemoaning how she was taken from us. Five years along, we still thought of Bethany every day, but we were also getting on with our lives. We did not deny that our lives had become very different, but it was life, nonetheless.

Death can be most tragic in the effect it has on those who do not die. We have known others who seem to be permanently stuck in their grief. We determined, however, that we would not become professional victims. We asked God to help us to become not only survivors, but overcomers, even transformers.

We learned from Bethany that, no matter what the source of our loss and no matter what we have experienced, what lies ahead is directly related to our attitude. We can choose to define ourselves by our loss and spend the rest of our life in grief and anger, or we can choose to get through it, trusting that God still has good in store for us.

Bethany was only seven years old, but she was a good teacher. We're still trying to be good learners.

In another column, almost three years later, I described what I considered to be a significant date. I had worked it out carefully, first in my head while driving, then rechecking with a calendar to make sure it was right. The day was November 30, 2002, and it was the 2,873rd day after Bethany's death. The number was significant (to me, at least) because her life on this earth had ended just 2,873 days after it began, fifty days short of her eighth birthday.

When November 30, 2002 arrived, we had lived without Bethany for the same amount of time we had lived with her. And I noted that it still hurt, though the pain was not so near the surface as it was. By God's grace, as the years go by, our memories are tinged more with quiet smiles than with bitter tears, with sweetness rather than salt. It is a gift of God, the ability to move beyond sorrow to find healing and wholeness and hope. It is a gift of God that comes with time, often mediated by the gifts of God's people who remind us that they remember, too.

The proximity of the date to Advent and Christmas reminded me of how trying the holidays can be to those who have lost loved ones during the past year. Memories come crashing back. The extra space under the tree cries out for presents neither bought nor given. It hurts, and there's no way around it.

I reminded our readers that friends can make all the difference—just by understanding, by remembering, by reminding the mourner that they remember, too. For someone who is hurting, there is no better gift, and Christmas is not a season for stinginess.

The ninth anniversary of Bethany's death proved to be yet another step in a lifetime of moving on, as I finally moved Bethany's bicycle from the garage. We had cleaned out Bethany's room a little less than a year after her death, and donated most of her things to a local charity. But I couldn't let the bicycle go.

The frame was mostly bright orange, with splashes of purple. The tires were white, and Bethany thought that was special. A vinyl pouch on the handlebars collected the stuff she found interesting, mostly rocks. She had customized the bike with a small tag behind the seat and colorful plastic sliders from a cereal box on the spokes.

I remember how proud she was when the training wheels came off and she made her first two-wheeled loop around the cul-de-sac, with countless others to follow. Often, she was leading a parade of other children on their bikes or roller blades or "Hot Wheels" trikes. Bethany loved that bike, and I loved watching her ride it.

And there it sat, long after Bethany's departure, as I cleaned out the garage to make room for Samuel to fashion a neighborhood "clubhouse." There it sat, with tires nearly flat, the paint fading, her dusty helmet still hanging from the handlebars by the chinstrap, the vinyl pouch still bulging with rocks she had picked up here and there. At last, it seemed, the time was right, and I put the bike into the truck with the yellow bus full of Duplo blocks that Samuel had outgrown and with the bags of clothes and other donations for Goodwill. When I carried it in, a young employee took the bike and wordlessly rolled it away.

I managed to avoid crying as the bike disappeared into the back of the store. I hoped that some little girl would enjoy it, that she would ride hard and laugh hard, rattle the spokes and scratch the tires. She wouldn't know the bike's story, and we would not know her story, but it was time for the bike, like us, to play another day.

As the tenth anniversary of Bethany's death approached, Jan and I had been working on this book and feeling Bethany's absence more than we had in years. Thoughts of the looming day were a tangible weight on our spirits. We could have observed the day alone, accompanied only by dark thoughts. We chose instead to share the day with others who had walked with us from darkness into light, inviting them to drop by our home for a time of reminiscing and to receive our thanks for the many ways they had encouraged us through these years. We remembered happy times and painful times, and it was a good time.

One friend brought photographs she had taken at a party when Bethany was just three and a half years old. She had lined up the dozen or so children at the party for a picture. Knowing that they would probably make goofy faces, she told the children to make funny faces for the first picture, then asked them to smile for a more typical pose in the next one.

Bethany did the opposite, making a funny face in the second picture. We laughed, and it was okay.

✳

Jan

My personal journey toward healing made particular progress as I completed a unit of Clinical Pastoral Education (CPE). I had long wanted to do the basic unit of CPE in order to explore ministry avenues in a hospital setting as a chaplain. During fall 2002, I was accepted into the program at Wake Medical Center in Raleigh and often worked in the same trauma unit where Tony was treated following the wreck.

For three months I worked as a chaplain, dealing with trauma patients in the emergency room or consulting with their families, and visiting with patients who had orthopedic and neurological illnesses. The time proved therapeutic for me as a person and also gave me the opportunity to enter the lives of others who were dealing with loss, pain, and grief.

In the short three months of the program, I felt that I did more ministry with those I encountered in the hospital than at any other time in my life. My own grief experience did much to enhance the depth of my ministry with others. I found it personally reassuring to know that I could enter and share the pain of those facing grief and tragic situations. I became, in the words of Henri Nouwen, "a wounded healer."

During the basic unit of CPE, I encountered patients and family members who struggled with some of the same questions I had pondered when Bethany died. Why did this happen? Why didn't God prevent this? Where was God?

I knew what it was to be angry with God and to question God's actions. Following Bethany's death, there were some who sought to answer such questions and to justify God's work and intention for our lives. We heard the familiar sayings: "God won't put any more on you than you can bear." "God has a reason for Bethany's death." "This was God's will." "God doesn't make any mistakes."

I have learned that there are no answers to some of the questions I asked God to answer. It does not dishonor God to ask such questions, but over the past few years I have come to feel less need to ask them. I came to believe that the God I served did not go about killing little children with trucks driven by drunken drivers. Bethany's death was the result of one person's choice to drink and drive. God gave all of us the free will to make choices. Sometimes those choices are good and sometimes they are horrible, even deadly.

God had nothing to do with Bethany's death. I believe that God's heart broke the moment Bethany's heart stopped beating. God was present with Bethany when she died and God has been present with us since that time. I rest in the thought that when it comes my time to die, I will be reunited with Bethany in heaven. At that time, the questions will not matter.

I have learned that the grief process is hard. Shock, numbness, and denial serve as a cushion to get us through those first days of the raw pain. A necessary emotional release can bring some relief. The following days and months can bring periods of isolation, physical distress, guilt, and depression. As the days turn into years, acceptance and hope can be known.

I went through many of the classic stages of grief, though in no particular order. Like Tony, I found that the journey through grief is cyclical. We may think we are through one phase, only to find that some event or memory will send us reeling back to an earlier stage of grief. I found it most helpful not to fight or flee, but to work through the feelings that each stage conjured up along the journey.

It took almost two years after Bethany's death before I finally felt that I had returned to the land of the living. I have gone through periods of depression during the past ten years and have felt waves of grief engulf me at unexpected moments. I have learned to assimilate Bethany's death into my daily life, very aware of the hole in my heart, but living nonetheless.

There are reminders each day that Bethany is no longer here. Sometimes the memories are sweet and sometimes the memories are painful. I have learned that the depth of pain her absence brings is but a reminder of the depth of my love for her. When we love someone deeply, we also grieve deeply when that person dies.

I will forever be grateful to family members and the many friends who surrounded us with love and care when Bethany died. The greatest gifts came in the form of presence and patience from caring individuals who never sought to explain our grief away. They plunged with us to the depths of our grief and rejoiced with us when we took baby steps toward hope and healing. They were true ministers of God's grace and love, even when they didn't know what to say. A hand held, a warm embrace, an errand run, a memory shared were all expressions of care and concern that touched me deeply.

I have come to know that I do not have to live as a victim. I have chosen to live with the death of my child in a different way. We were victims of the horrible choices another person made on that cold January day. Nothing can change that fact. But we have the choice in how we live our lives in the midst of tremendous loss and pain.

It would have been easy just to lie down, to say that life was not worth living without Bethany. I could have wallowed in my grief and harbored the anger and bitterness I felt toward Darrell. I could have blamed Tony for the wreck and added to the guilt he was already heaping upon himself. I could have ceased loving others to avoid the pain of grieving when they died. I could have blamed God and walked away from a life of ministry and service. Those choices would do nothing to honor the memory of Bethany or bring healing to my heart.

I have learned that I have power to overcome, to forgive and move forward. I have experienced every parent's worst nightmare and lived to tell the story. Though I have been the recipient of the consequences of one person's choice to drink and drive, I have not let that determine the quality of my life. Bethany's death will not define me as a victim, nor will I choose to live as one. I am a survivor, a person with a deep reservoir of strength, faith, and hope that continues to sustain me today.

That is not to say that the loss is forgotten or that I have fully recovered. One never fully recovers from the loss of a child, but abundant life can be known. There is life after the death of a child.

I can smile and laugh. I can sing and feel joy. I can love and be loved. I have survived and continue to thrive. I have learned to remember, not what we lost as a result of Bethany's death, but how blessed we were to have Bethany for seven short years. I have found that even in Bethany's death, there is life.

Getting Over and Getting Through

Tony and Jan

As we have worked our way through these years, we have often come into contact with others who have faced the death of a child, spouse, parent, sibling, or close friend. Still facing the empty darkness, they ask, "How do you get over it?" Or they may be more concerned with a variation on the same thought: "When do you get over it?"

Sometimes friends or acquaintances who can only imagine the death of a child will ask the same questions, curious to know how one gets over the loss of someone so precious. And our response is consistent. "You don't get over it," we say. "You learn to get through it."

Just as forgiveness is an ongoing process, not a one-time thing, coping with loss is a lifetime project. You get through it by trusting God to be with you, even in the darkest nights.

You get through it by hoping against hope that the sun will shine again, that God can work in you to create something good from the pieces that are left.

You get through it by allowing friends to walk with you, talk with you, and speak openly about loss as well as hope.

You get through it by acknowledging your feelings, accepting them, but not always being governed by them.

You get through it by recognizing that grief is cyclical and by learning to be patient when waves of grief come crashing down and it seems that you're back at the beginning.

You get through it by making choices, day after day, that you will not surrender to victimhood. The tragedies or losses you face may be deep, and they will almost certainly not be fair. The death of a loved one may leave you with an emptiness as real as winter rain and as dark as a cloudy night, but seeds of hope can sprout if we let them. Life can begin anew. It will be a different life, but it can still be a good life, one that honors the dead not just with grief, but with growth.

This is a promise from God, who is faithful and true. This is something we learned from Bethany, who still touches our hearts. And we are immensely grateful for both.

Description of Cover Art

The cover art for this book draws on elements of a painting Bethany did in art class not long before her death. At the time, we thought little of it beyond admiring her work and taking note of the various themes she had incorporated into the picture (see a black and white reproduction of her painting on the previous page).

Looking more closely at the picture after Bethany died, we came to see it as bordering on the prophetic. The bottom of the picture is pure Bethany—bright colors and trees, green grass, friendly animals, creepy critters, and a happy fish in a pond.

The middle part of the picture is unexpectedly muted in color, split by what appears to be a lonely road over a high hill. A stormy purple sky populated by ominous "m" birds and sharp lightening bolts broods over the wooded land beyond.

Flying free above the foreground is a bright bird of red and blue, winging its way out of the picture.

We came to think of ourselves as travelers on the lonely road from "Bethany land" to the dark country beyond the horizon, catching an occasional reminder that the child we cherished was no longer earthbound. In a very real sense, though in different ways, both Bethany and we had entered a whole new world.

STUDY / DISCUSSION GUIDE

BY STEVE SUMEREL, NCC

introduction

The following guide is designed for use by a designated leader or facilitator. This book can be a wonderful resource for those who are in the midst of a loss. "Option 1" questions are designed for use with group members who are still working through the loss of a loved one. "Option 2" questions are designed to help a general audience understand their role as friends and comforters to those in grief, as well as helping them prepare for their own future journeys through the grief experience.

This is a deeply personal book that took courage for the Cartledges to share. All the questions and suggestions in this guide are designed to help readers to apply the Cartledges' story to their own lives. Every attempt is made to avoid asking group participants to judge the actions of Jan and Tony; instead, participants are encouraged to use the book as a mirror to reflect their own thoughts and feelings.

Each group session begins with prayer. Certain suggestions for prayer remain constant throughout the book, with specific prayers relating to aspects of the chapter.

"For Further Thought and Reflection" is designed for those who are truly searching for additional guidance or ideas for journaling their personal reflections during their grief journey.

Leaders may encourage participants to journal their own journey through this book. You will note in the discussion guide for chapter 10 that there is a time to reflect on lessons from the whole book. It would be appropriate at that time for participants to share from their journals to the degree they are comfortable.

Steve Sumerel is executive director of the Council on Christian Life and Public Affairs of the Baptist State Convention of North Carolina.

chapter one

Opening prayer time
- Pray for each individual in a specific way.
- Pray that God will use your gathering and this book to meet the needs of the group.
- Pray for awareness and thankfulness for the ordinary, and courage and strength for crisis.

Preparing for Discussion
Lead the group in a summary of chapter 1. You may want to use the following:

Throughout their book, Tony and Jan tell their view of the story separately. Perhaps this approach was a natural extension of the harsh reality of death. Encounters with death are inherently lonely. No one can experience your own death for you, and no one can grieve a loss in your place.

The story begins with Jan and Tony at far different places. Not only were they in two different states; more importantly, they were at two different points of involvement in the unfolding tragedy. Tony was present, making decisions, becoming part of the tragedy itself. Jan was far removed, completely at the mercy of an event unfolding beyond her reach.

Discussion Questions
Option 1
(1) As you think about your own loss, whose story most reflects your experience?
(2) Did Tony's stark proclamation, "I chose wrong," reflect any feelings of guilt or responsibility in your loss?
(3) Caring friends surrounded Jan when she received the news of Bethany's death. How did you find out about the death of your loved one? Did you have anyone with whom to share the experience?
(4) Life is often predictable. How do we react when the unexpected and terrible befalls us?

Option 2
(1) Whose story would you most fear to be your own?
(2) Even though the driver of truck clearly caused the crash, how do you understand Tony's statement, "I chose wrong"?
(3) Tony was intentional in selecting who would tell Jan about the tragedy. How would you tell someone such news? How would you prepare yourself for such a task?
(4) The Cartledges' tragic day promised to be normal and predictable. How does one prepare for the unthinkable?

For Further Thought and Reflection
There is much we can control, and there is much we must leave totally in God's hands. Reflect on and write about the concerns in your life and who has control of them. Pray for strength to deal with the things that are in your control and wisdom to let go of the things that are not.

chapter two

Opening Prayer Time
- Pray for each member of the group specifically.
- Pray that God will use the group to further the journey of each participant.
- Offer a time of silence. Have the group use this time to ask their most
  haunting questions to God. Offer a time specifically to listen to God's
  response.

Preparing for Discussion
Lead the group in a summary of the chapter. Ask what made the most
impact on them. Perhaps the following synopsis will be helpful in reflecting
on the chapter:

> Tony could not physically be at Bethany's funeral, so it was important
> to him for his thoughts to be shared during the service. His words sent a
> clear message of how he understood God's place in this tragic event. Jan was
> haunted by endless unanswerable questions and her longing to touch,
> soothe, and communicate with her daughter. Both Jan and Tony spoke of
> well-intentioned comforters and how their actions were received.

Discussion Questions
Option 1
(1) Reread the text of Tony's letter that was read at Bethany's funeral. How
    do Tony's words reflect (or not) your feelings of where God is in the loss
    of your loved one?
(2) What questions continue to demand your attention? Are you waiting
    for answers or learning to live with the questions?
(3) If your loss was that of your child, how have you dealt with your need
    to continue to be a parent?
(4) What did your supporters do that brought the most comfort to you?

Option 2
(1) At what points did Tony's letter push your faith?

(2) How can you respond to those who are asking unanswerable questions?

(3) How comfortable are you when you have no clear answers to questions?

(4) From the Cartledges' story, what have you learned about comforting those in grief?

For Further Thought and Reflection

It is an age-old question: "Where is God is the midst of pain and suffering?" Reflect on and write about your present understanding of this question. At what point do you still feel stuck in your understanding of God's presence in difficult times?

chapter three

Opening Prayer Time
- Pray for each member of the group specifically.
- Pray that God will use the group to expand each participant's wisdom.
- Have the participants recall a time when they felt particularly close to God. Invite them to imagine themselves at that time.
- Offer a time of silence for each participant to seek that closeness again. (For those who cannot recall such a time, offer them an opportunity to invite God to be close to them now.)

Preparing for Discussion
Move into a discussion of the chapter by reminding the group of areas Jan and Tony covered. Use the following synopsis if you desire:

In this chapter both Jan and Tony speak of the incredible pain they suffered. Like the empty chair at the kitchen table, anything can become a stark reminder of how invasive the loss is. However, they also spoke of the unexpected sources of comfort. Tony found comfort in sharing stories of Bethany and in hearing "A Whole New World" in a whole new way. Jan, faced with the "impossible" tasks of choosing clothing for Bethany, choosing the casket, and other tasks that truly were the ultimate challenge of parenting a deceased child through burial, found profound meaning and comfort in the shooting star.

Discussion Questions
Option 1
(1) What are/were the invasive reminders of loss you have encountered?
(2) What were the serendipitous moments of comfort?
(3) What were the hardest tasks you had to do during your time of loss?
(4) Where did you find the strength to do these tasks?

Option 2
(1) What thoughts or feelings did you experience as you read this chapter?

(2) Friends were heroic in their ministry with the Cartledges. Have you ever been privileged to play such a role? What was your experience?

(3) Christopher's gift was profound in its purity. What gifts are yours to offer in a time of grief?

For Further Thought and Reflection

Whether it was through music or the flash of a shooting star, God broke through incredible pain with His presence. Reflect on those experiences in your journal or in your prayer time. Can you attach these past experiences to a promise of God's presence in the future?

chapter four

Opening Prayer Time
• Pray for each participant specifically.
• Pray for guidance in facilitating this group.
• Pray for peace and rest from the hard work of grief.

Preparing for Discussion
This chapter covers many important aspects of the grief process. Ask the group what part of this chapter gave voice to their own experience. Use the following synopsis to cover areas the group might not mention:

This is a chapter of contrasts. While Tony recuperated from his injuries, his thoughts turned to the nature of heaven and his renewed interest in knowing more about it. Jan was far from contemplating heavenly things, dealing with the red tape of death and the mountain of details of keeping the home fires alive. However, both began facing special days for the first time without their daughter, observing that their path through grief was not nearly as linear as Kübler-Ross describes in her books.

Discussion Questions
Option 1
(1) Recall the first special days following your loss. What was this like for you?
(2) Tony shared images of heaven that brought him comfort. Have your thoughts of heaven changed since your loss? What concepts about heaven bring you comfort?
(3) Jan confronted the loss of a future together. How did your view of the future change following your loss?
(4) Jan's poem not only expresses her experience, but it helps others grapple with their own losses. Reread Jan's Mother's Day poem, paying attention to your feelings. What do you experience?
(5) If you were to draw your journey through grief, what would it look like? Is your path straight, winding, or circular?

Option 2

(1) Many people alter their concept of heaven following the loss of a loved one. What is your understanding of heaven? What has informed this view?

(2) Tony and Jan remind us how important family members are during special days throughout the year. Did reading this chapter give you a renewed awareness of special people, especially on special days?

(3) Jan's Mother's Day poem covers the gamut of a mother's relationship with her daughter. Which part of the poem stands out in your mind? Why?

For Further Thought and Reflection

Usually our understanding of heaven develops as we mature and especially as we experience the deaths of those we love. Write about or reflect on how your understanding of heaven has changed over the years. Toward what is your image of heaven moving?

chapter five

Opening Prayer Time
• Pray for each participant specifically.
• Pray that God will be in the midst of the discussion.
• Pray that each participant will be present and patient with one another.

Preparing for Discussion
Prepare for the discussion by summarizing the main points of the chapter.

Like Job's comforters, many well-intentioned friends tried to defend God's plan in Bethany's death. Such attempts only added to the Cartledges' despair. In response, Tony offers an insightful article in which he outlines three "P's" of being helpful as a friend to a grieving person: presence, patience, and purpose. Jan comes to the decision to seek professional help from those trained in the use of these three P's.

Discussion Questions
Option 1
(1) When was a person's presence the most meaningful in your loss? When was it most significantly missing?
(2) When was a person's patience the most meaningful in your loss? When was it most significantly missing?
(3) Jan bravely faced the choice of seeking professional help. Was there a time in your grief when you were compelled to ask for help? What do you need to ask for now?
(4) Tony spoke of things he learned from his experience. What are your most significant lessons of the heart?
(5) Some feelings are just too painful to experience. What do you need to help you meet the challenge of such intense pain?

Option 2
(1) Tony helps us understand how important it is to know your purpose when visiting a person in grief. Does his insight change how you prepare to be with a grieving friend?

(2) Tony shares three things that moved from his head to his heart—the absolute ugliness of sin, the centrality of Christian hope, and the ultimate importance of human choice. What has been your experience of these truths?

(3) What experiences have helped you move ideas from your head to understandings of the heart?

For Further Thought and Reflection

Sometimes it is not easy to ask for the help you need. Write about or reflect on the barriers you encounter that keep you from asking for the help you need. What do you need to overcome these barriers?

chapter six

Opening Prayer Time
- Pray for each individual in the group.
- Pray that God will use this time in which you gather together.
- Using David and Goliath as a guiding metaphor, offer a time of silence when the participants can visualize themselves confronting the giants standing in the way of their progress.
- Ask: What is God saying to you as you confront these giants?

Preparing for Discussion
Summarize the chapter using the following synopsis:

In this section Tony and Jan are like David confronting Goliath. Their battles with insurance companies and the justice system were experiences of frustration that prolonged the grief process. They also confronted Darrell's entrenched defense system that protected him from taking responsibility for his actions.

Discussion Questions
Option 1
(1) What have been the Goliaths of red tape that have frustrated your path through grief? Do they remain obstacles?
(2) Are there ways you have found to navigate through legal systems that you would like to pass along to others?
(3) Tony and Jan wanted Darrell to take responsibility for his actions to help them move on to forgiveness. What were/are the obstacles for your journey toward resolution?

Option 2
(1) Do you think there are ways that red tape can be reduced in the time following a person's death? If so, in what ways?
(2) Do you have knowledge or experience that can help a grieving person through the legal systems that follow a death?

For Further Thought and Reflection
A will is a gift to those who survive you. Reflect on and/or write about your own will, last instructions, etc. What more can you do to prepare others and yourself for your own death?

Opening Prayer Time
• Pray specifically for each group participant.
• Pray for God's presence in the group process.
• Offer a time of silence in which you invite the participants to reflect on the following: God is present throughout the year, even a difficult year. How does God make His presence known in spring, in summer, in autumn, and in winter? Give participants time to consider each season for a while.

Preparing for Discussion
Offer your own or the following synopsis of the chapter to prepare the group for discussion:

This section speaks to the power of memories. Jan and Tony recount the struggles and rewards of the first year after Bethany's death, as each special day brought significant pain and healing. Tony also describes how the amazing presence of Fred Rogers became an integral part of their story.

Discussion Questions
Option 1
(1) Reread Tony's "Memorial Day." What would you include in this poem from your own story?
(2) Fred Rogers played a significant role in the Cartledges' recovery. Who broke through your grief in a significant way to help you glimpse God? What did this person say or do? What aspect of God's love did this person help you experience?
(3) Each special day prompted Tony and Jan to remember Bethany in a meaningful way. How have you experienced this? How have you used special days to move you toward a more peaceful place?
(4) Writing Mr. Rogers a note of thanks was the beginning of a wonderfully redemptive story for the Cartledges. Are there those to whom you need to say "thank you"?

(5) When unexpected death occurs, it becomes easy to take on the role of victim. Has this been a struggle for you? Who are your role models for shaking off this role?

Option 2
(1) Who has most exemplified the presence of Christ in your life?
(2) What are some ways you can be God's presence in the life of a person in need?
(3) Jan spoke honestly of the hostility she felt toward Darrell. What is it like for you to be present with someone expressing such feelings? What do you think you would have said to Jan during this part of her journey?
(4) Read Tony's Memorial Day poem, and reflect on its meaning in your life.

For Further Thought and Reflection
This chapter was about special days. As a creative exercise, consider this: What if there was a holiday in honor of your loved one or in honor of your family? What would the holiday be called? When would it be celebrated? What special things would people do on this day?

chapter eight

Opening Prayer Time
- Pray for each participant in your group.
- Pray that God will be in the group process.
- In a time of silence, encourage your group to envision a picture of what they hope for in the future. What choices will they need to make for this future to come? How can God help them in moving toward this positive future? Give your group time to ask God for help and time to listen.

Preparing for Discussion
Use the following or your own synopsis of the chapter to begin the discussion:

One of the most significant choices Tony and Jan made after Bethany's death was their decision to have another child. Coming out of the fog of the first traumatic months, they began the process of establishing a future.

Discussion Questions
Option 1
(1) Have you made a major life choice since your loss? May the group hear about it?
(2) How did you know you were ready for such a choice?
(3) The "journey" is seen as a useful metaphor in this section. Can you see your story as a journey? Draw a verbal picture of your journey.
(4) The teddy bear was an object reflecting grace and was a useful transition object in Tony's journey toward recovery. Do/did you have an object that offered comfort in some significant way?

Option 2
(1) Tony shares some lessons about prayer in this section. What was the most significant new insight you gleaned from his reflections?
(2) Tony helps us understand that listening is an important aspect of prayer. How can you best listen to God?

(3) Small things like a medicine bottle or major events like the birth of a child can trigger unexpected waves of grief. How can you help a grieving person through these times? (Often, the person going through this feels stuck or unhealthy because they feel they are losing ground.) How would you pray with/for them?

For Further Thought and Reflection

Continue to reflect on and/or write about your future. Are there major forks in the road ahead? What do you need to invest in now to be where you want to be in the future?

chapter nine

Opening Prayer Time
• Pray for each person in the group.
• Pray for God's felt presence within the group.
• In a time of silence, offer participants an opportunity to explore areas in which they need to forgive and/or seek forgiveness.

Preparing for Discussion
Tony's intense work on the books of 1–2 Samuel gave him time to ponder the powerful parallels of his story and that of King David and his children. Jan's narrative reaches a wonderful climax of forgiveness as she rids herself of the toxic effects of anger and resentment.

Discussion Questions
Option 1
(1) What biblical narrative best parallels your time of grief? How has this narrative informed your journey?
(2) Has your loss altered your understanding of any of the biblical stories? What are some new perspectives you bring away from your journey?
(3) Jan had a long wait for the pieces needed for forgiveness to come together. What do you need in order to move along on your journey?

Option 2
(1) Although Jan's story is unique, everyone has issues of forgiveness in their lives. What did you learn about your own experience through Jan's story?
(2) Tony identified with King David. With whom in the Bible do you identify? What experiences have shaped your understanding of this biblical character?

For Further Thought and Reflection
Just as Tony found profound parallels within the pages of the two books of Samuel, reflect on and/or write about the biblical narratives that parallel your story.

Also, Jan found incredible restoration through the process of forgiveness. During this week, pray and meditate on these words of the Lord's Prayer: "Forgive us our trespasses as we forgive those who trespass against us." Ask God for new windows though which you can see new insight in this well-worn verse.

c h a p t e r   t e n

Opening Prayer Time
• Pray for each member of the group.
• Pray for God's meaningful presence in the group and in its process.
• Offer a time when participants can reflect with God, ask God, or thank God for their experiences with this book and this group.

Preparing for Discussion
As they conclude their book, Jan and Tony come to hard-won conclusions. They acknowledge the importance of what their daughter taught them about themselves, and accept the clear invitation to explore all areas of life and death more fully. Throughout their book, the Cartledges tell their stories separately. However, they end in unison—a reminder that it was their two voices telling one incredible story.

Discussion Questions
Options 1 and 2
(1) What part of this book will you keep closest to your heart?
(2) "You don't get over it; you get through it." These words introduce the summary of the Cartledges' lessons. Borrowing from the Cartledge story or your own, discuss what you have learned about dealing with grief. What experiences bring these lessons to life for you?
(3) During the course of this book study, participants have been given an opportunity to reflect on their own story. Give the group time to share how the themes of the book touched and/or changed their own lives.

For Further Thought and Reflection
It is hoped that this book has given you a good start on the rest of your journey. As you continue on your path, continue to give prayerful consideration to your own story of life and faith.

APPENDICES

What about the Children?

BY JANICE HAYWOOD

The Day After the Wreck

Bethany was a prominent participant in the church's children's ministry, so when the adults met on the evening after the wreck to pray and share their grief among friends, the question of what to do with the children emerged. The first suggestion was to continue with the regular Wednesday evening programming, but the children were grieving, too, and they had many questions. They had seen their parents' grief and had learned various amounts of information about what had happened. Their parents felt inadequate to answer some of their questions. For many of the children, this was their first experience with death, and almost no one had experienced the death of a friend.

We decided that the preschoolers would continue with their regular classes, but the elementary-age children would be brought together for a joint session. We had a general outline for the session, but we also knew that the children needed to ask their questions and share their feelings. We moved the classroom furniture so that we could sit in the middle of the floor in close proximity. The room was quite full, so it was an intimate gathering.

Since I was the only one who had done any study about how to explain death to children, I was the person who led the session. I had flown in from out of state only that morning, and I, too, was reeling with my own grief and questions. However, the children needed help, and I was willing to do the best I could to help them through this difficult time. Children often are excluded in grief experiences because we want to protect them, but they need to be heard and included even if we don't have all of the "right" answers.

I began by telling them in simple terms exactly what had happened in order to clarify some misinformation several of the children had pieced together from what they had overheard. I simply explained how the wreck had happened, where it had happened, and that a man had made a bad decision to drink alcohol and drive a car, and he caused a wreck that killed Bethany and hurt Mr. Tony. The children had questions that I tried to answer honestly without going into detail, partly because I did not know all of the details and also because they did not need to know some of the information about the aftermath of the wreck. I concluded by reminding them that sometimes we can make bad decisions that will hurt others, so we need to ask God to help us make good decisions that please Him.

The children reacted with a wide range of emotions. Some of the younger children in particular expressed little feeling but sat very close to an adult, and a few children were fearful for many days. Many of the children were crying, and several of the older children were very angry. We let them express their feelings and assured them that it was okay for them to feel that way.

I thought it was important to explain the emotions they saw being expressed by their parents and teachers. I acknowledged that they had seen and would continue to see the adults crying. We were very sad because we loved Bethany and would miss her. (Even as I shared this with them, the adults in the room, including me, had wet eyes.) I explained that our tears were for ourselves, not for Bethany because she was with God in heaven and she was happy and doing great.

Next, I explained what they would see when they went to the funeral home, assuring them that they could choose to go or not to go. Since many of the children had never been to a funeral home or service, I gave a lot of detail. I told them that Bethany's body would be in a "box" called a casket, but "who Bethany was inside" was with God. I told them she would not be breathing or opening her eyes. I assured them that they could hug Ms. Jan and tell her anything they wanted or say nothing at all. I told them that Ms. Jan, their parents, and their teachers could use lots of hugs (and I knew they did, too).

I also told them about a funeral. The service had not been planned at this time, but I explained that it would be like going to church on Sunday except that we would be remembering Bethany. I shared the kinds of things they might experience and once again assured them that they could choose to attend or not attend.

We prayed for Mr. Tony and Ms. Jan (and for us), and then we gave the children the option of making cards for them. Most of the children jumped right into the activity, but some children continued to ask questions or express their emotions.

The Funeral Home Visitation

Another woman and I stationed ourselves at the closest point where the parents and children would see the casket before turning to speak to Jan and the other family members. Many of the parents were overwhelmed with emotion, so we tried to comfort the children as well as the parents. The children talked about the body not looking like Bethany, why were there so many flowers, and various other observations and questions. Many of the children hugged us, ministering to our grief while we were trying to minister to theirs. Several of the children brought roses, stuffed animals, and other remembrances that we put in the casket for them.

The Funeral

When we were planning the funeral service, Tony and Jan expressed a desire to have a time with the children, since the children were used to being included in our worship services each Sunday. I was asked to lead that time and knew that it would be the most difficult "children's sermon" I had ever done. We decided to make it a time of remembering things about Bethany that they liked. I talked to as many parents as I could so that they could prepare the children ahead of time. I suggested that they could write their thoughts and hand the paper to me, or they could share them out loud.

When that time came in the service, the children gathered with me at the front of the worship center next to the casket, and they shared many memories of Bethany—some written and some verbal. We closed by attempting to sing "A Whole New World" with a tape, despite the tears of the children and adults alike.

I am grateful that we included the children in the entire experience. Sometimes we try to shelter children from death because we think it is too painful for them (or us). When children are included and are given assurance and comfort, they begin to accept death as a part of life.

Through the years, as the children have become older, they have continued to process the experience through their more mature understanding of death. They generally remember it as a helpful, community experience that bonded them with the church family in a powerful way.

Additional Suggestions for Helping Children

Preschoolers, who do not understand the nature of death, will reflect the feelings of the important people in their lives. Often they cry because you are crying, not because they are sad about the death. If the preschooler does not seem to be recovering from the loss, check your own emotional state because preschoolers live in the present.

You will not be able to hide your feelings from children—they are very perceptive even when we think we are being good actors. Older preschoolers do not need to experience the depth of your grief, but they do need to be included in discussions about being sad. You can help them begin to express their feelings with words rather than acting out feelings with inappropriate behavior. Be empathetic of their feelings and let them draw pictures of the person who has died. Often they can draw a picture of how they feel when they do not have the verbal skills to communicate it.

Preschoolers do not understand the permanence of death and view it as a temporary separation. Because they are largely illogical thinkers, they often do not understand logical explanations. It is important not to say things such as "Grandpa has gone to sleep" or "God wanted Bethany to be with him." They may be afraid to go to sleep or become angry with God for taking their loved one away. Say what it is (dead or death), and repeat it whenever the preschooler brings it up. Assure them of the dead person's love for them and that they are with God in heaven.

The death of a pet can be a helpful "first experience" as you explain that they can no longer run, jump, breathe, or eat. Depending on the child, you might have a funeral and burial.

Elementary-age children begin to understand that death is final, inevitable, universal, and personal. Many of them become fearful of death because they fear the deaths of their parents, themselves, and other important people. Handling death appropriately is important at this age (following the "standards," rituals, and proper procedures), so they will ask questions. They are curious about the details of funerals, caskets, vaults, graves, and cremation, for example. This knowledge is one way of feeling that death is not something mysterious but rather a process with rules.

It is best if they can first experience the funeral of someone with whom they do not have a close relationship before they experience it with someone important to them. It is common for children to feel anger toward the dead person, think that they may somehow be responsible.

Older children have a better understanding of right and wrong, and this sometimes leads them to view death as punishment for misdeeds. For example, they may have thought Bethany did something to deserve death. The older child moves from thinking of death as an external power to an internal dysfunction that causes life to end. Even in the case of a wreck, they may think death comes as a dysfunction of the body.

While these are some general age group guidelines, each child will react differently to death experiences. Answer their questions honestly and include them in the grief experience as much as they want to be included. Some children will not want to go to the funeral home and/or funeral, and I believe you generally need to respect their wishes. Remember that as they grow up, they will continue to process the deaths they experience in childhood.

Janice Haywood is Senior Consultant/Coach for Congregational Services and Team Leader for Preschool and Children's Ministry for the Baptist State Convention of North Carolina. She is also adjunct professor at the Campbell University Divinity School.

When Death Comes to the Youth Group

BY HAL MELTON AND JAN CARTLEDGE

One Group's Experience

Bethany was a special friend to the teenagers at Woodhaven Baptist Church. With Jan serving as minister of youth and education, Bethany was with the youth group frequently, especially during the summer months for weeklong mission trips and youth camps. The youth considered Bethany their "mascot," a title she cherished. Needless to say, the youth were shocked and saddened by Bethany's death.

The youth were not strangers to dealing with death. Two years prior, the teens had ministered to a boy in the group whose father died from cancer. Two months prior to Bethany's death, a sixteen-year-old member of the group had been killed in a car wreck. The volunteer youth leaders and teachers learned through these experiences that youth aren't as equipped to deal with death as adults, and they tend to deal with their grief in different ways. The youth had already been confronted with the reality of death and the possibilities of their own mortality. They now needed comfort and assurance again, as the reality of Bethany's death began to settle upon them.

The youth leaders and teachers decided to gather the youth in one place so they could begin grieving together. Hal Melton provided the playroom in his home as the meeting place for the youth group on the evening after the accident. This gathering in a safe place gave the teenagers an opportunity to offer support and comfort to each other, to cry and to share.

Knowing that the teens would be curious about how, when, and where the wreck had happened, Hal and other leaders shared honestly what news they could about Bethany's death and Tony's injuries. It was important for the youth to hear the facts, to know the truth, and to begin dealing with the impact on their lives.

The youth were a tight-knit group. They were used to sharing openly and deeply as friends, so when the opportunity was given for each one to share their feelings, the floodgates opened and words and tears broke through. Emotions ran the full scale of humanness, from anger at God and hatred toward the drunken driver to tear-streaked laughter as they remembered precious moments spent with Bethany. The adult leaders were willing to let the youth voice their feelings and emotions and were careful not to offer any judgments about anything the youth said.

After this time of sharing, Hal read Tony's note that he had written to the Woodhaven congregation. The note opened up a new level of sharing as the youth and adult leaders wrestled with Tony's observations versus other views they had heard from family members or other ministers. The youth expressed a belief that Bethany's death would definitely cause them to consider the possible consequences of their actions in the future more deeply than they had ever done before. The youth and adults also affirmed that Bethany's death and Tony's observations would call them to examine what they believed about God's will, human free will, and failure.

The youth signed a card that was later sent to Tony while he was in the hospital. They then talked together about ways they could personally and collectively minister to Jan and Tony in the days, weeks, and months ahead.

The youth and their leaders took a giant leap in "growing up" spiritually and emotionally as a group that evening. They left the meeting knowing that the Woodhaven church family and the youth group would never be exactly the same again. Bethany was gone. Jan and Tony would need the church family and God in ways they had not even discovered yet, but the youth would be ready and willing to minister as those needs became clearer in the days to come.

In the days leading up to the funeral, the youth found many ways to express care and love for Jan and Tony. Several of the youth visited with Jan at her home, bringing warm hugs and words of comfort. Some youth just came and sat on the couch and held Jan's hand for a while. Others wrote Jan and Tony letters, sharing words of comfort and special memories of Bethany. Many of the teenagers went to the funeral home visitation, and some brought flowers or notes to put in Bethany's casket.

On the day of the funeral, the youth group sat together in the choir loft. Their faces were some of the first Jan saw when she entered the sanctuary for the service. It was a sign of their unity and shared grief and a wonderful gift of presence and support for Jan and her family.

Suggestions for Helping Youth

The openness, honesty, and love shared on the evening following Bethany's death proved to be an important time for the youth and their adult leaders. The adults were able to assure the teenagers that it was okay to cry, to be sad, and to be angry. The teenagers were reminded that they were not alone in the journey of grief. They gained strength from one another and learned both the joy and pain that comes from caring deeply for others.

When death comes to a youth group, adult leaders are encouraged to be present and available to the teenagers. Provide a safe place for the youth group to gather together and to share their hurt, sadness, and stories. Encourage the teens to write a letter, make a card, or find other meaningful ways of ministering to the grieving family.

Remember that teens will not all grieve in the same way. While some youth were able to visit with Jan in her home, others did not feel comfortable doing so. Some youth were vocal with their feelings, while others were silent. Be attentive to teenagers who might need some extra help in dealing with their grief, especially if there is a noticeable change in their usual habits, schoolwork, or if they become isolated or depressed. Some youth may also turn to drugs or alcohol or other destructive behaviors in an attempt to cope with the pain and loss. A trusted counselor with expertise in dealing with adolescent grief might be needed to help through this time.

For teenagers needing another avenue of expression through the grief process, you could encourage them to begin writing in a journal as a means of expressing their deepest feelings and remembrances. Writing poems or songs can give creative expression to the emotions a youth might not be able to verbalize aloud.

The youth group could also create some type of memorial as a tribute to the person who died. The Woodhaven youth group planted a tree in memory of Bethany. Others have raised funds for a charity in memory of their friend or found other tangible ways of expressing their care. These can be beautiful reminders of the life and growth that can come to our lives, especially in times of loss and grief.

Hal Melton is Associate Pastor at Trinity Baptist Church, Raleigh, N.C.

Select Bibliography of Grief Resources

Bernstein, Judith. *When the Bough Breaks: Forever After the Death of a Son or Daughter.* Kansas City: Andrews McMeel Publishing, 1998.

Bowen, Deborah, and Susan Strickler. *A Good Friend for Bad Times: Helping Others through Grief.* Minneapolis: Augsburg Fortress, 2004.

Claypool, John. *Tracks of a Fellow Struggler.* Waco: Word Publishing, 1974.

Heegaard, Marge Eaton. *Coping with Death & Grief.* Minneapolis: Lerner Publishing Company, 1990.

Hipps, Richard, ed. *When a Child Dies: Stories of Survival and Hope.* Macon: Peake Road, 1996.

Rosof, Barbara. *The Worst Loss: How Families Heal from the Death of a Child.* New York: Henry Holt and Company, 1994.

Sanders, Catherine. *Surviving Grief . . . and Learning to Live Again.* New York: John Wiley & Sons, Inc., 1992.

Strommen, Merton and Irene. *Five Cries of Grief.* Minneapolis: Augsburg Fortress, 1996.

Wolterstorff, Nicholas. *Lament for a Son.* Grand Rapids: Eerdmans Publishing Company, 1987.

Resources for helping children

35 Ways to Help a Grieving Child. Portland: The Dougy Center for Grieving Children & Families, 1999.

Cave, Anne Good. *Balloons for Trevor.* St. Louis: Concordia Publishing House, 1998.

Fitzgerald, Helen. *The Grieving Child: A Parent's Guide.* New York: Fireside, 1992.

Huntley, Theresa. *Helping Children Grieve: When Someone They Love Dies.* Minneapolis: Augsburg, 1991.

Johnson, Joy and Marvin. *Children Grieve, Too: Helping Children Cope with Grief.* Omaha: The Centering Corporation, 1998.

Mundy, Michaelene. *Sad Isn't Bad: A Good-Grief Guidebook for Kids Dealing With Loss.* St. Meinrad: Abbey Press, 1998.

Silverman, Janis. *Help Me Say Goodbye: Activities for Helping Kids Cope when a Special Person Dies.* Minneapolis: Fairview Press, 1999.

Resources for helping teenagers

Dower, Laura. *I Will Remember You: A Guidebook Through Grief for Teens.* New York: Scholastic, Inc. 2001.

Fitzgerald, Helen. *The Grieving Teen: A Guide for Teenagers and Their Friends.* New York: Fireside, 2000.

Grollman, Earl. *Straight Talk About Death for Teenagers: How to Cope With Losing Someone You Love.* Boston: Beacon Press, 1993.

Helping Teens Cope with Death. Portland: The Dougy Center for Grieving Children & Families, 1999.

Traisman, Enid Samuel. *Fire in My Heart, Ice in My Veins: A Journal for Teenagers Experiencing a Loss.* Omaha: The Centering Corporation, 1992.

Devotional resources

Becton, Randy. *Everyday Comfort: Readings for the First Month of Grief.* Grand Rapids: Baker Books, 1993.

Miller, James. *Winter Grief, Summer Grace: Returning to Life After a Loved One Dies.* Minneapolis: Augsburg Fortress, 1995.

Wunnenberg, Kathe. *Grieving the Loss of a Loved One.* Grand Rapids: Zondervan, 2000.